The Last Farewell...

A guide to devising the content and format of a Funeral Ceremony

Dorothy Shorne

No part of this publication may be reproduced without prior written permission of the publisher. Ceremonies may be replicated for individual or celebrant use.

Note that Australian English is used in this book, and will vary in places to spelling used in the United States. Some terminology may be unfamiliar to readers outside of Australia.

Recognition is given to the
sharing of ideas and concepts
by fellow celebrants.

Second Edition printed April 2025
Copyright © Dorothy Shorne
ISBN: 978-1-7640472-0-3

Cover Image: DepositPhotos
Cover Design: Winsome Books

Winsome Books
Adelaide, South Australia

Contents

Introduction 1
    Location 3
    Costs 4
What Happens When Someone Dies? 7
Funeral Format 10
    Working with the Funeral Director 11
    Suggested Order of Funeral Ceremony 14
Writing The Eulogy 16
Possible Rituals 18
    Candle Ceremony 19
    Placement of stones for a Girl Guide leader. 20
    Bell and flowers at the time of committal 21
    The Ode for a Veteran 22
    Spiritual Ritual 23
Sample Ceremonies 25
    Ceremony for Angela 25
    Funeral for a child 31
    Funeral for a Loner 38
    Funeral for a Difficult Person 42
    Interment of Ashes 44
    Memorial Service 46
    Suicide 46
    Pet Funerals 49
    Special Interest Funerals 53
Music which may be used for a Funeral or Memorial Service 54
Poems and Readings 56
Check list of who to advise 67
Further Reading 69

Dedication

In memory of my mother, my sister, and my father, whose funeral ceremonies I have conducted in that order.

Those occasions were emotionally difficult, but I coped because of the advice of fellow celebrants, and the information that I had access to within these pages.

Foreword

Two separate books are combined within this publication for reader convenience. The first, **The Last Farewell**, provides guidance for someone who is tasked with arranging a funeral, possibly at short notice. It also serves as a resource for the new funeral celebrant.

The second book is **It's Your Funeral**, and as the title suggests, it guides the reader through the steps to take in planning their own funeral. It offers the chance to take charge of this very personal farewell, and ensures that stress is minimised for those left behind.

Together, each book provides the information needed to deliver a funeral that meets the needs of the deceased, their bereaved relatives and friends, and those who have come to pay their respects.

Dorothy Shorne

Introduction

I was appointed as a marriage celebrant in 1995, and after a couple of years, began receiving requests to preside over funerals. This was a quick learning curve in providing ceremonies for people of all ages, including babies, and for those who had died of natural causes, from unexpected events, or through suicide.

Families handle their grief in different ways, there are various venues in which a funeral or memorial ceremony can take place, and different funeral directors have their own way of doing things. At all times I have needed to be flexible, to practice the art of diplomacy, and to be a good listener in compiling a ceremony that meets the needs of the bereaved.

This book will assist those who want to be involved in arranging or delivering a funeral ceremony, either as a celebrant or for someone close to them. It will also assist a new celebrant who is seeking further information and assurance. Any religious ceremonies will follow the format dictated by the particular church or religious belief, but some suggestions within this book may also be incorporated within a religious funeral.

❈

"What should I do now?"

These are the words that might flash through your mind when confronted with the loss of a loved one. It is an overwhelming time. Not only are you confronted with your loss and your own emotions, but you have to slide into organising mode, contacting friends and relatives, appointing a funeral director, and making other arrangements.

If this is an anticipated death, it is possible that the deceased has thought about this day well in advance and has left instructions about the order of service, who to include, and what music to be played. This information may be stored in the same place as a copy of their will, or left with a trusted person.

In relation to advance planning, people don't need to be ill to take this step. Many people like to be organised, to retain a measure of control until the end, and to make the time easier for those they leave behind. Leaving instructions is a step I advise for anyone when the subject arises.

The process is similar for both a funeral, where the body or the ashes of the deceased is present, or a memorial ceremony which may take place a period of time after the person has died. This can also be called a Celebration of Life Ceremony.

This book outlines the format for a non-religious ceremony, but any funeral may include religious elements, whether they be a reading of the *Lord's Prayer*, or an extract from the Bible such as John 14:2. There may be elements pertaining to other religions as well, or even Pagan or Wiccan inclusions. What is important is that the wishes of the deceased are recognised, and the needs of the bereaved are also met. A ceremony may be spiritual, even though it is not a religious service.

A civil service follows the same general format as any other, except that the wording is a little different. Rather than being religious, the wording for a civil ceremony is based upon the life of the person who has died, constituting a biography or eulogy.

It is a flexible service, which allows for the inclusion if desired of different speakers, the playing of music, and the reading of verse or other material of relevance. A funeral service can be held at a variety of locations. It could be at home, in the rooms of a funeral parlour, in the chapel at a crematorium, at the graveside, or even in a garden or some other location that was meaningful to the deceased. If the funeral party is to proceed from a service location to a cemetery, words of committal are said at the final destination.

Don't let anyone rush you into the funeral. It is quite acceptable to take a few days to think about what you want and to organise it. You can have your choice of funeral celebrant, not just the one supplied by the funeral director. You can also not have a funeral celebrant if you wish, but can organise the tributes collectively with close friends and family.

The benefit of engaging the services of a good celebrant is that there will be someone to act as MC, to coordinate speakers and participants, and to smooth out any sticky bits. They will also help to manage the conflicting emotions that can arise both in the preparations and on the day.

Location

It is not necessary to hold the ceremony in a chapel. You can choose a community centre, a special garden, or any other venue that seems appropriate. Even the local scout hall. The benefit of having another venue is that you have more flexibility. The chapels must be booked, and unless yours is the last ceremony of the day, you must adhere to a strict time schedule. They may (though not necessarily) be impersonal.

Check that if you choose an alternative venue, there is easy access for the coffin (i.e. no stairs, or those that are easily negotiated). If it will also be the location of the wake, ask what kitchen facilities available. What catering items are included– crockery, cutlery, glasses, urns, etc. With some venues, you will need to hire these items.

If you hold the funeral in a venue of your choice, you can have the ceremony and then flow on into the celebration of life party, i.e. the wake. The deceased does not need to be removed immediately after the ceremony. This gives people time to make their personal farewell. Have some photos around or other items of relevance to their life. When you are ready, you can ask the funeral director to take the deceased on the next phase of their journey. Keep in mind that you will be paying for the funeral director's time.

Costs

Some costs associated with a bereavement and funeral will be unavoidable. There will be:

- A death certificate
- a coffin or casket, whether conventional or a woven basket, etc.
- Funeral Director's fees
- Cremation fees if cremation is chosen
- Cost of a plot, and cemetery fees if interment is chosen
- Other costs if another method of disposing of the body is available.

Conventionally, the funeral director collects the deceased and transports them as required, and keeps them in their mortuary until the day of the funeral. They will organise other things such as booking a chapel, placing notices in the local papers, printing funeral cards, coordinating any audio-visual requirements, and organising catering. They may also prepare the body for the ceremony through embalming, doing hair and make-up, and dressing in the outfit that has been chosen (or a shroud).

There is a cost for those services, and there are obvious benefits in having everything taken care of in a time of grief and stress. The deceased may even have made financial arrangements in advance for these costs to be taken care of.

If cost is a major consideration for you, or retaining control is important, the funeral director does not need to do everything for you. You can undertake some tasks if you wish. You can order flowers independently, or just pick them from your garden. Mourners may also bring flowers.

You can choose a very basic coffin and cover it with a favourite cloth, quilt, item, children's drawings, etc. Don't feel pressured into choosing something more elaborate if that is not what you want. You can even get an unpainted coffin, and which the family or friends can paint and decorate it as desired. It is a simple matter to design and print the memorial cards, if you have access to appropriate software and a colour printer.

Ask guests to bring a plate of food and bring some cut flowers from their garden. (Take plenty of vases or jars). Make it a simple and meaningful event. People will appreciate being able to contribute to the day. Appoint someone to coordinate the flowers and another to accept delivery of the food.

If, through circumstances, you are required to have two events, you can have a small intimate ceremony first, and then a memorial service a week later with the ashes, or even just a photo of the deceased. The only consideration in this circumstance is that it draws it out the process for you.

This book will assist anyone who wants to plan in advance, or those who have the planning of a funeral thrust suddenly upon them. It can also be used as a reference text for funeral celebrants as they guide their clients through the process of organising a funeral.

The Last Farewell

What Happens When Someone Dies?

If you are reading this book because you have to organise a funeral now, you will have already encountered the information in this chapter. You can skip and read the Funeral Format advice instead. For those who are approaching this topic with a view to being better prepared when the time comes, read on.

If someone has died in unusual circumstances, or in situations such as dying within a certain time period after being released from hospital, the coroner may be involved. The police will be advised by the attending medical personnel, and they will take a statement from others who were present at the time of death, or who discovered the deceased. The body will then be removed in the coroner's van. The coroner will establish whether an autopsy is required, and also when the body can be released. State-based legislation will dictate the circumstances under which a death must be referred to the coroner.

If someone dies whilst in ongoing medical care, such as in a hospital, or when under the active and recent care of a medical practitioner (as defined by legislation), the death is not usually referred to the coroner. In this situation, the funeral director of choice can be contacted and they will remove the body for safe-keeping at the mortuary until the day of the funeral, assuming there is to be one.

Before the deceased is removed, the family will usually have the opportunity to spend some time with them, to come to terms with the passing, and to make their initial and private farewells. Hospitals and other institutions will usually only summon the funeral director after allowing the bereaved the dignity of this time.

The death must be verified on the designated form by an authorised person before the body is removed. This form will be used to notify the Office of Births Deaths and Marriages that the death has occurred, with a request for registration to take place and a death certificate to be issued. Typically, the funeral director will perform this administrative duty. Note that procedures may vary from state to state, depending on the relevant legislation.

The funeral director will make a subsequent appointment with the bereaved to discuss preferences and arrangements for the funeral. That will cover what services you want the funeral director to provide (printing of memorial cards, arranging audio-visual presentations, publishing death and funeral notices, etc.) as well as discussing the type of coffin or casket required, what clothing the deceased should wear, and whether embalming is required. Discussions on the venue will also address the catering requirements.

Preferably before, but if not during this meeting, the bereaved parties will have discussed their preferences for how and where the funeral might be held, what type of ceremony they want, who they want as a celebrant, and what functions will be provided by family and friends.

The celebrant can be someone recommended by the funeral director, or can be an independent person chosen by the bereaved. Sometimes, people will choose a celebrant who has previously provided services to the family, such as being their marriage celebrant, or conducting a prior funeral. If belonging to and active in a particular faith, the bereaved may choose to engage a religious celebrant.

The celebrant will usually meet separately with the family to discuss the structure of the ceremony and to gain the information for the eulogy. Sometimes the celebrant will write the eulogy from the details provided, and sometimes, one or more mourners will deliver the eulogy instead.

The choice of music and readings will be discussed, and opportunities for other people to be involved in the ceremony. There is scope for people to speak, or perform another function such as the lighting of a candle, singing or providing a musical recital, or participating in another ritual of farewell.

At the conclusion of the funeral ceremony, the mourners may proceed to the cemetery in a procession if a burial is to take place. In this situation the funeral director will have liaised with the owner of that cemetery to have the grave site excavated in preparation for the interment. The plot may have been purchased prior to this particular death, or may have been quickly organised in the days prior.

A brief ceremony of committal follows, and the funeral director will supervise the lowering of the coffin or casket, and will liaise with the cemetery employees. Occasionally, the complete ceremony will be at the graveside.

If the body will be cremated rather than interred, the funeral director will transport the deceased to the crematorium at the conclusion of the funeral. Occasionally, the chief mourner may also wish to accompany the body on this final journey and observe the process, but this is not common.

Mourners usually adjourn to the wake at the completion of the funeral, either within the funeral parlour, or at some other designated venue.

Funeral Format

Music may be played while mourners are taking their seats in the place of ceremony, or is used as the opening statement. The celebrant (or MC) will open the ceremony, welcoming the mourners and giving the opening words of address. They will reflect on the deceased, and what that person meant to those present. There may be a reading or a verse of relevance after this introduction.

The eulogy follows. This a history of the deceased's life and major influences – family, schooling, work, life choices, interests, little quirks, favourite stories, personality, etc. More than one person may contribute to the eulogy, perhaps referencing different segments of the deceased's life. Often, others present are also invited to speak, but that depends on the time available for the ceremony and the location.

Those who speak in an impromptu basis are likely to be succinct. Others who have been requested in advance to speak may ramble. If there is a time limitation, it helps to indicate to speakers the length of time available i.e. five minutes each, and suggest to them that they write their thoughts in dot points at least to maintain focus on what they want to say. Some will write it out in full.

Children may also participate. They could write a letter, a poem, or a story. If they are nervous about speaking in front of the audience, someone else can read the written words while the child stands nearby. Much laughter often comes with the sharing at this time, but of course some tears as well. Make sure a box of tissues is handy for those who are speaking.

The Last Farewell

After the speakers, the celebrant will refer to the comments that have been made and briefly summarise any key points. You may then listen to some reflective music so that people have a few quiet minutes to think about their relationship with the deceased. The music does not have to be sombre, and an audio-visual presentation may also be played at this time.

This may be followed by another reading, and then the celebrant will draw the ceremony to a close with words of committal and farewell, and will advise on what is happening next – stay for refreshments; move to another venue, or whatever. There can also be some closing music to the formal part of the day. The tone of that music ranges from upbeat to solemn. Some suggestions are provided later in this book.

You can change the ceremony format around as much as you like. You can include singing, more impromptu activities, provide an audio-visual display, include rituals of relevance, and decorate the hall with symbolic items, etc.

If presiding over a small, intimate funeral, the mourners may prefer to gather in a semi-circle. This draws people closer together and involves them on a more personal level. Whether or not this is feasible will depend on the location, and the set-up of the venue.

Working with the Funeral Director

Celebrants and the funeral director are part of a team, and they need a good working relationship in delivering the funeral ceremony. They may have never worked together before, so meeting or at least having a phone call before the ceremony is advisable.

The funeral director will need to know:

- What music has been selected, usually around three tracks;
- Who is supplying the music, and in what format;
- Is an audio-visual display planned, and who is providing the photos or other material and when. Most funeral directors have contacts who can take the raw material and develop it into a display. They will also have the necessary equipment to use on the day;
- Are there any particular rituals or events that are planned within the ceremony?

The celebrant will need to know:

- How much time is available for the ceremony (some chapels will be booked for a specific duration);
- How this particular funeral director prefers to open the ceremony.
  - Usually, the coffin or urn has been delivered to the chapel in advance, and is in position for where it will stay throughout. At the appointed time, the celebrant moves to the lectern at the front of the hall or chapel and proceeds with the opening
  - Other times, the coffin may already be in place, but the funeral director and/or arrangers, and the celebrant proceed to the front of the room in solemn procession after all the mourners are seated.
  - Less common, but another option is that the coffin is carried in after all the mourners are seated, with

the funeral staff and the celebrant following behind;

- Process for the end of the ceremony.
    - If a cremation will follow the funeral, there may be a button to press on the lectern, that lowers the coffin marginally. This is a symbolic action. The coffin is not descending out of sight.
    - Mourners, with family and chief mourners invited first, may step forward and place a sprig of rosemary, flower petals, or other material on the coffin. Usually, the funeral arranger will come forward with a basket containing those sprigs, etc. and mourners will take one as they file past. The mourners then proceed out of the chapel and continue to the place where the wake will be held.
    - If the funeral is held in a hall or garden or other non-chapel location, it is possible that the wake will occur in the same place and the coffin will remain for a while before being removed for the final journey.
- There will be announcements at the end of the ceremony relating to what will happen next, and where people should go after paying their last respects. Either the funeral director or the celebrant can make that announcement, but that needs to be clarified between them.

Suggested Order of Funeral Ceremony

1. Announcements:
   - Format of the occasion
   - Turn phones to silent or switch off.

2. Introduction:

3. Poem or Reading:

4. Eulogy/biography
   - Other speakers

5. Poem/Reading

6. Reflective Silence
   - Music
   - Prayer

7. Announcement:
   - Where to proceed next, if applicable.
   - Invitation for refreshments

8. **Cemetery or Graveside**

   There may be a procession of mourners, following the coffin and pallbearers to the gravesite.

9. Music (optional) Could be a piper, other instrumental, or a vocalist.

10. Opening words of address (some people may attend who were not at the earlier ceremony)

11. Poem/Reading: (optional)

The Last Farewell

12: Words of Committal

The lowering of the coffin will occur in coordination with the funeral director. It should be discussed and agreed in advance at what point in the proceedings that this occurs. Usually, the celebrant will make eye contact with the funeral director at the appropriate time. The coffin may be only partially lowered, and then fully lowered after mourners have departed.

At the conclusion of the ceremony, mourners may step forward to drop sprigs of rosemary, flowers, or handfuls of soil onto the coffin.

This format is flexible, and can be adapted to accommodate the requirements of the deceased (if known) or the bereaved.

Writing The Eulogy

After a careful interview to record all the pertinent facts, the eulogy can be written and presented to the bereaved for approval and verification of all the details, including names and dates. It is possible that friends or family members may like to contribute to or write the eulogy themselves. The following dot points serve as a guide to the issues that might be covered.

They are not all-inclusive, and there may be additional anecdotes or memories that you would like to have included. It is not necessary that all of the dot points are covered – they are presented as suggestions only.

- Name
- Date of Birth
- Place of Birth
- Parents, Brothers and Sisters
- Early life and family, parent's occupation, early home life, childhood interests, areas in which the family lived.
- Education – Primary, Secondary, Tertiary
- Trade/Profession
- Courtship/Marriage
- Children and Family Life
- Places where family lived/work places
- Personality/ characteristics/ sense of humour
- Community Service
- Achievements
- Beliefs
- Causes

The Last Farewell

- Political Ideals
- Recreation/ Sports/ Hobbies
- Likes and dislikes – Music, the Arts, Poetry, Literature, Television, Radio
- Travel
- Animals
- Illness and cause of death
- Any other relevant information.

The eulogy may be delivered by the celebrant, or by a friend or relative. Different people may address different aspect of the eulogy, i.e. one may talk about family matters, and a work colleague may talk about events in the work place.

Possible Rituals

Items can be placed on a memorial table, in a position where they can be referred to at various times during the ceremony. Later, the items can be transferred to the wake. Those items are usually a range of objects or mementos that of significance to the deceased or the family. It could be a favourite photograph, or a piece of craft work, or a piece of favourite clothing.

In a similar vein, when my mother died, we ordered a very simple coffin, but covered it in a quilt that she had recently made for a granddaughter. It was a fitting tribute to her many crafting interests.

While on the topic of coffins, my father drove VW Kombi vans for decades. For him, my siblings and I requested a cardboard coffin that was screen-printed in a Kombi design. He would have been tickled pink to see it. Other people have ordered plain, unvarnished coffins and painted them with motifs, etc that reflected the interests of the deceased. Often many people were involved in the decorating process, allowing them a proactive role in the grieving process.

Symbolism is important. If you would like candles, flowers or other items to play a role, that can be accommodated within the service. Take your time to think about what you would like, and how you would like to celebrate the life of your loved one.

These are a few of the rituals that have been included in funerals I have conducted.

The Last Farewell

Candle Ceremony

Family was important to Mary and of course she was to each of you. Marking that important relationship, I would like to ask each of the grandchildren to step forward to light a candle for their grandmother, adding a few words of what Mary meant to them.

Susan, I now ask you to come forward and light the first candle for your grandmother.

Four Candles

First Candle is lit – Susan to come forward and light the candle
The first candle represents our grief,
The pain of losing you is intense.
It reminds us of the depth of our love for you.
Susan to add a line of special memory of how Jenni demonstrated her love for her grandchildren.

Second candle is lit – Jason to come forward and light the candle.
The second candle represents our courage,
To confront our sorrow,
To comfort each other,
To change our lives.
Jason to add a line about something special that Mary did that made a difference to everyone's lives.

Third candle is lit – Natalie to come forward and light the candle.
This third candle we light in your memory,

For the times we laughed,
The times we cried,
The times we were angry with each other,
The silly things you did,
The caring and joy you gave us.
Natalie to add a line of about a humorous memory.

Fourth Candle is lit - Annie to come forward and light the candle.
This fourth candle, we light for our love.
We light this candle for you so that your light will always shine.
As we enter this sad time and share this day or remembrance
with family and friends
we cherish the special place in our hearts
That will always be reserved for you.
Annie to add a line of special memory – one of the things that she will always remember about her grandmother.

Mary, we thank you for the gift your living brought to each of us.

Anonymous

Placement of stones for a Girl Guide leader.

When the Girl Guides take their leave of a camp, it is traditional to leave a series of stones behind in a special pattern, indicating they have been there and have gone home. Members of the Girl Guides of SA will now make their farewell to Ann, incorporating this unique ritual.

The Last Farewell

Guides come forward to place a stone on the coffin, before collectively singing 'Taps' (along with other Guides who are present).

Bell and flowers at the time of committal

(Can be adapted for other situations)

This ceremony was in a park on a sunny morning. As the deceased had died overseas, it was a memorial ceremony. Central to the circle of mourners was a wide glass bowl, on which were several floating candles, which were lit at the beginning of the ceremony.

Music fades and celebrant rings a small bell.

We remember today the life of the man who has influenced Jackson with his love, and who will continue to impact on who Jackson is and what he does. Like the sound of a bell resonating in the welcoming air, Alan has resonated in the lives of Jackson, Henry and those around him. (*ring bell again*)

We commit Alan's hopes and ideals into our minds and our wills; his loves we commit to our hearts; his spirit we commit to the world at large, and his body we commit to its natural end. Jackson, will you now step forward and cast the flower upon the water.

The Ode for a Veteran

There are prescribed procedures if members of the Returned and Services League (RSL) participates in the ceremony of a veteran, and they can be found on the RSL website. Other countries will have similar advice in relation to services for veterans.

The scope of that involvement will vary according to the location and scope of the ceremony, and of course the wishes of the chief mourners. Options may include the placing of the national flag on the coffin, a guard of honour comprising other serving or ex-servicemen, and instead of flowers or sprigs of rosemary, red poppies may be placed on the coffin.

At the end of the ceremony, but before the committal, the Last Post may be played, usually with a recording but occasionally with a bugler. The following words are then read, either by a military person, or failing that, by the celebrant.

> They shall grow not old,
> As we that are left grow old,
> Age shall not weary them,
> Nor the years condemn,
> At the going down of the sun,
> And in the morning,
> We will remember them.

Everyone repeats: We will remember them.

Celebrant: Lest we forget.

Everyone repeats: Lest we forget.

The Reveille is then played, after which the red poppies are handed out for placing on the coffin.

The Last Farewell

Spiritual Ritual

This ritual recognises the elements of earth, fire, air, and water, and the spirits who influence those aspects of our lives. The supporting actions or elements can be varied according to what is practical or what is relevant. For instance, instead of a candle representing fire, an incense stick that has been lit could be used instead. Some venues may not permit candle flames inside. The use of this ritual calls for creativity.

Example

Simon was a child of the universe, with a respect for the earth and the elements. We send him on the next phase of his journey with the blessings of the spirits of north, south, east and west and the blessings of the elements of our common being – earth fire, air and water.

Celebrant holds a candle aloft.

(North) Spirit of Fire, we thank you for passion, for courage for cleansing. Hail and farewell.

Celebrant waves a feather gently over the casket.

(East) Spirits of Air, we thank you for clarity and memory. Hail and farewell.

Celebrant lifts a handful of earth.

(South) Spirits of Earth, we thank you for receiving back the body of Simon and for nurturing us in life. Hail and farewell.

Celebrant dips fingers into water and sprinkles some over the casket.

(West) Spirits of Water, we thank you for clarity and memory. Hail and farewell.

Note that in the northern hemisphere, the Spirit of Fire is located to the south, and the Spirit of Earth is located in the north.

Sample Ceremonies

The following ceremonies will give an idea of how the ideas and suggestions described in earlier pages might be applied.

Ceremony for Angela

Pachabel's Canon in D to be playing as guests are entering the Chapel.
Family and friends – good morning. On behalf of the family of Angela Ambrose, I thank you all for joining them, and sharing in this opportunity to salute a life well lived.

Our coming together is an occasion on which we draw close not only to give solace, but to commemorate, to celebrate, to mourn and to support. This is the community that comprised Angela's world–her family and friends, their friends. There are also those with whom she either gave or received support over the years. Though we will mourn her death, this is a time to remember and acknowledge the life that Angela lived.

With this ceremony, we recognise the loss that we have all suffered in varied and personal ways. Today you may reflect on those memories and perhaps you would like to share some of them with others, if not at this ceremony, then later in the day.

Angela was a person who played an important part in your lives and has left a lasting impact - in your memories, in the stories shared, in the tears you have cried and of course the laughter. The loss of a mother, a grandmother or a friend leaves a gaping hole in your heart and but there is a finality now that is irrefutable.

Angela quietly slipped away on Monday 5th May, just a couple of months short of her ninety fifth birthday. She is survived by daughter and son Linda and Peter, grandchildren Allan, Pauline and Katie, and great grandson Austin. She is also mourned by Linda's partner Bruce, Peter's partner Carol, and Austin's mother Lorna, as well as her friends and extended family from Adelaide, Melbourne and Port Macquarie. Recent months were spent at Gentle Rose Nursing Home at Glenunga and the family appreciates the love and care that both Angela and the family received during that time.

Peter and Linda recall that their mother loved dancing. Husband Laurie was perhaps not as keen, but in all things, they supported each other. The following reading is appropriate therefore as we focus on the woman that Angela was.

(Poem read, Many Winters, by Nancy Wood)

Although she lived in Adelaide for most of her adult life, Angela was born in at Cowell on Eyre Peninsula, one of four siblings. From Peter and Linda, I have learnt a lot about Angela's life – her early days, her life with Laurie, her sociable nature, her love of a good card game, and the fact that she was always immaculately and stylishly presented. Perhaps the cards were a feature of her early life as the family lived initially away from city distractions on a rural property, before moving to the Barossa Valley. The family would have made their own entertainment.

Her first job was an office appointment at Sheard's department store in Nuriootpa, which was an important regional focal point in those days. At twenty-one, she made the bold move to the city and boarded with the Smiths, a family with whom she retained strong contacts. It was in their home also that she met Laurie, who was to become her future husband. I believe that she was a popular young woman and had many suitors but Laurie was the one who won her heart and hand.

Coming from a hotel family, Laurie was a publican and ran the Royal Hotel at Glenelg. The hotel featured strongly in the lives of the young family, as Angela and Laurie were soon joined by Linda and then Peter. Many of the children's early memories incorporate events and activities at the pub.

Laurie also was intimately involved in the thoroughbred racing industry, owning and racing many winners–and probably some losers. Although racing was not a particular interest of Angela's, she accompanied her husband as the horses were taken to various events, in South Australia and interstate.

After Laurie retired from the hotel industry, making his move before the advent of late-night closing, he continued his involvement in property development and investment, and even their family home on Fisher Street contained a small flat. This was occupied by various tenants and the friendships made were retained over the years.

The years without the restrictions of the hotel made it easier for Angela to indulge her interest in travelling, and she made the most of it. Being a very sociable person and a good networker before it became an acknowledged art form, she made a lot of friends during her travels and subsequently visited many of these people in their home countries.

In her middle years, Angela developed her interest in painting, acquitting herself with some skill. You will see an example of her artwork on display here today. In her later years Angela was spotted by a talent scout, and recruited as a model. She was always well-turned out as the photos that are on display attest, and thoroughly enjoyed the many modelling gigs that came her way. With the current focus on older people remaining an active part of the workforce, it is refreshing to see that a woman post-thirty was sought for this role.

The woman I have learnt about is one who was very sociable and who had a generous nature. She enjoyed company and took life as it came, enjoying the moment and sharing what she had. I have given a brief synopsis of a long and fruitful life, but members of the family will share more personal memories. Linda and Peter would like to tell you about their mother.

Eulogy delivered by Peter and Linda

Other family members may speak and the invitation to be extended to those present.

And so sums up a full and rewarding life. We can see how this woman touched many with whom she came in contact. Our experiences and our times with her were similar, but each unique, leaving us with our special memories. Others may care to take this time to reflect on the meaning that Angela's life had for them. The music that is played for us at this time is a compilation of her favourite singers.

Music: Compilation track

The separateness, the uniqueness of each human life is the basis of our grief in bereavement. Look through the whole world and there is no one like the one we have lost. Angela still lives on in all our memories and, though no longer a visible part of our lives, she will always remain a member of

The Last Farewell

our family or of your circle, through the influence she has had on us all.

The value of that life is not measured in years, though if it were, we could say that Angela's life was worth a lot. The meaning of life can be understood in the manner of living it, and living it well. Angela lived each day thankful for what she had, and thankful for her family. She drew pleasure from her friends, her social activities, and the fact that life was good.

I invite Lucy Hammond to step forward and sing Amazing Grace.

Lucy Sings

I draw this ceremony to a close with the words written by a fellow celebrant, Maggie Dent and titled 'Sometimes'.

SOMETIMES
Sometimes on our journey through life, we meet people
Who leave footprints on our mind
They challenge us to see things differently
And to question our personal reality.
Sometimes on our journey through life, we meet people
Who leave footprints on our hearts
They create a safe place for us to open our hearts
To feel loved and special.
Then sometimes on our journey through life, we meet people
Who leave footprints on our souls
They share themselves with us so profoundly that they touch
The very essence of who we are in that secret quiet place.
Angela has left gentle footprints on the minds, hearts and souls of many here today.

May we always remember, the beauty of her love,
The kindness and the sacred way she touched our lives.
Maggie Dent

We commit Angela's hopes and ideals into our memories; her loves we commit to our hearts; her spirit we commit to the world at large, and her body we commit to its natural end. We are grateful for a life that has been well lived, and for all that this life has meant to us.

Thank you all for coming and sharing this day and the memories. Rest in Peace Angela. I invite you to step forward to make your farewells, beginning with Angela's family, and whilst you do, the background music will be 'Dream the Impossible Dream'. Refreshments will be served in an adjoining room and you are invited to join the family for a glass of champagne in honour of a life well-lived.

Music Plays. Mourners step forward to pay respects, and then adjourn to the refreshment room.

Funeral for a child

Funerals for children are always emotionally challenging. As a celebrant, it is important to read the ceremony text aloud in private, possibly a couple of times, in order to be in command of the words that are to be delivered. The occasion will be heavily charged with emotion, and that affects the celebrant as well. You will never be de-sensitised to this situation, but it will help to manage your own emotional response on the day, when those in front of you are understandably weeping copiously. Staff from the funeral director may be reaching for the tissues as well.

If a baby or very young child dies, or does not survive the birthing process, the parents may like to include a naming ritual within the funeral ceremony. This acknowledges the existence of their child, and confirms that the baby was and continues to be a member of their family.

The parents may like to display relevant items on a table, such as photos, favourite toy, a pair of booties, or other item of significance to the family. Those items can be mentioned as part of the ceremony. Guests may be asked to each bring a flower (can be of a particular colour, though not necessarily) which are placed around the tiny casket as a floral tribute.

Clothing worn for funerals is often restrained, but for a child's funeral, black may not be appropriate. The family may have a specific request in relation to clothing and colour, so discuss the options with them.

Ceremony 1
Ceremony to honour the cherished life of Alison Gail Boston

A Mother's Love
I didn't have to look into your eyes
To fall in love with you.
I didn't have to hear you cry
To know you loved me too.
I didn't need to hold your hand
To cherish you always.
Within my womb we shared our hearts
You touched my soul
You sweetened my spirit
You gave me memories I'll always
Hold very dear
Yes, my heart aches since
You departed so soon
But a mothers love does not
End with death
For you are my child
my love is forever yours.
　　　　Author unknown
Sourced from www.irisRemembers.com

Today we come together to honour the cherished yet fleeting life of baby Alison and also to say goodbye with great sorrow. This occasion acknowledges the precious love and joy with which Caroline welcomed the conception of Alison and her twin brother James.

The news of Caroline's pregnancy was a delight to those who knew her, all of us realising the tremendous personal journey that she undertook to make it happen. This pregnancy, with all the hopes that it entailed, was a source of much joy.

Although Alison's time with you was brief, Caroline, she will live on in your heart as long as you live, just as she would have if the little rosebud that was her life had blossomed into childhood and adulthood. She is now, and always will be, a part of your family and it is appropriate therefore that we take this opportunity to officially name her in the presence of you, her mother, and indeed you all.

Caroline, using this taper, I invite you to light your daughter's naming candle.

(Caroline is given a taper candle, which is then lit. She uses it to light the naming candle.)

We now bestow upon you the names of Alison Gail Boston. We give you your first name – Alison, this name honours your strength and sacrifice. We give you your middle name, Gail – this name gives depth and roundness and honours your community, being the name of your mother's dear friend. We give you your family name, Boston – this name gives you connection to those gone before and those yet to come. Your names will always be remembered and honoured.

When a woman finds she is pregnant she is transformed. She carries life within her and she is changed for all time. Caroline was expecting twins to be born on 15 August. Tragically, complications arose and after a long and mighty effort to stay, Alison was born too small, too soon on 15 April 2016. Caroline is devastated by the loss of her beautiful, strong baby girl. She mourns the fact that her brother James will grow up without his sister by his side. Instead, James will have a guardian angel watching over him.

When a child dies, we mourn not only the life that was, but also the life that would have been. It is right that we grieve, because sorrow is a reflection and measure of the love, the happiness and the intimacy that we shared with the one we have lost. We grieve for ourselves as well, because we know that the lives of those close to Caroline will not be the same without this little one. The death of a child touches everyone in a myriad of ways.

As we are gathered here to support Caroline, I would like to share a few thoughts with you. When faced with death, many of us worry about the right words to use - but there are no right words. There is no "right" way to act. Just be yourself. Speak from your heart - offer a gentle touch, or an act of kindness, or just simply show that you care.

There are so many ways of showing love, understanding and support; Just simply be there. I encourage you not to worry about saying the right thing but simply to be there for Caroline and her little family, not just for today, but throughout all the difficult times ahead.

Some people come into our lives and quickly go. Some stay for a while, leaving footprints on our hearts forever. Alison - you have surely left footprints on the hearts and lives of those gathered here today. You will forever be in the hearts of your loving mother and brother.

It is of some comfort to know that Alison will not be alone on this next journey. Grandparents Elsa and Peter and great grandparents Katie and Gavin will be watching out for their great granddaughter. A new little star will be shining down on us all from the heavens.

Light Second Candle for baby's soul, using the naming candle.

The Last Farewell

At the beginning of this ceremony, we lit Alison's Naming Candle. I now use it to light another that shines a guiding light for her on the path she now takes. Alison, we light this candle that your light will always shine through our sadness and share this day of remembrance. We cherish the special place in our hearts that will always be kept for you.

> **Snowdrop**
> *The world may never notice*
> *If a Snowdrop doesn't bloom,*
> *Or even pause to wonder*
> *If the petals fall too soon.*
> *But every life that ever forms,*
> *Or ever comes to be,*
> *Touches the world in some small way*
> *For all eternity.*
>
> *The little one we long for*
> *Was swiftly here and gone.*
> *But the love that was then planted*
> *Is a light that still shines on.*
> *And though our arms are empty,*
> *Our hearts know what to do.*
> *Every beating of our hearts*
> *Says that we love you.*
> *- Author Unknown -*

Tenderly and lovingly, we commit the body of this precious little child to the elements, and ultimately to Mother Earth from which all life comes, and to which, in the end, all life returns.

Alison: Go forth with love

Ceremony 2
Benjamin Smith

A photo is placed on a small table. As mourners enter, they are invited to place a tea light around the photo and to light it. Celebrant rings a bell a handbell.

To begin this ceremony, we light a candle for Benjamin. As you look at the light, think of the light that Ben has lit within you. The light of his spirit, the small flame that will burn forever, is your favourite memory of him. Think of the unconditional love that emanated from Ben. It was a unique love and without him, Whenever, you light a flame in his honour in the future, think of the unconditional love that was, and is, Ben.

There are no words of comfort that can cushion the shock experienced when one is faced with sudden and unexpected death. Even more so, when that death is the sudden death of a beautiful child.

Death in a number of ways unites us all. This child's death, for a time, demands that each one of us put aside our toil, our cares, our business, our pleasure, to unite ourselves with everyone here, who share in the common bond of love for Ben.

We grieve most for the passing of the young. If the old depart, we recognise a natural change, as when the sunset dissolves naturally into the dusk and the stars come out in the night. The death of a child shocks us as if the morning were suddenly overcast by blackness, the day suffering a dreadful eclipse.

This very grief is a token that death cannot take from us the most precious of our treasures – namely, Love. It is the tear

The Last Farewell

of love that flows the fullest, the pain of love that aches the deepest, the thoughts of love that move most actively.

For love is the very essence of the human heart; and when we are deprived of the child we love, our inner soul seems rent in two, and life is only a part of what it was.

The intense feeling of love that grieves for the young shows that nature itself is teaching us to keep hold of something that is truly worth the keeping. For of all memories the memory of the young moves us most deeply.

Poem, 'The Farewell' by Dolores Mae Wooley is read.

We give the care of this little one to the Universe and to Mother Earth from whom all life comes and to who, in the end, all life returns.

We are glad that we saw his face and felt the touch of his velvet skin. We cherish the memory of Benjamin. We know that thoughts of him will ever bring us comfort.

In token of our love for the young life that has untimely faded, let us resolve to offer a more generous affection to each other and, so far as we are able, to the young children of humanity the world over.

This life was no less dear because it was so brief;
The flower blooming for a day is just as fair as any tree in leaf;
The ray that lights a golden moment and is gone
Is just as lovely as the light that fills the day.
And this deep love locked close within our hearts,
Is one with that great love that holds us all.
      Dorothy Greenwell

We leave Ben in peace and bid him our fond farewell.

Funeral for a Loner

Some people die with no known next of kin, and possibly very few friends. Those who do attend the funeral may not know much about the deceased. This provides a challenge for the celebrant who is endeavouring to acknowledge the life of a recluse.

In talking about the cycle of life about someone for whom little is known of their life, you can always research what key events may have occurred in the year of their birth, and in the decades that followed, noting the changes that would have occurred in the world around them.

Ceremony for John

These words are from Ecclesiastes Ch 13:1-8

> *To everything there is a season,*
> *and a time for every purpose under heaven;*
> *a time to be born, and a time to die;*
> *a time for planting, a time for uprooting;*
> *a time for tears, a time for laughter;*
> *for mourning, a time for dancing;*
> *a time for searching, a time for losing;*
> *a time for conflict, a time for peace.*

We gather here with sad hearts to honour the life of John, the life of a man who in a small way, touched each of you.

Death is as natural as life: only Nature is permanent on this earth. All that has life has its beginning and end... and life exists in the time span between birth and death. Life's significance lies in the experiences and successes we achieve

The Last Farewell

in that span of time; its permanence lies in the memories of those who knew us, and any influence we have left behind.

Death is a very personal matter for those who know it in someone close to them. And we are all concerned, directly or indirectly, with the death of any individual, for we are all members of one human community, and no one of us is independent and separate. Though some of the links are strong and some are tenuous, each of us is joined to all the others by links of kinship, love, friendship, by living in the same suburb or town or country, or simply by our own common humanity.

The separateness, the uniqueness of each human life is the basis of our sadness when faced with death. Look through the whole world and there is no one like the one we mourn today. But he still lives on in your memories and, though no longer a visible part of your lives, he will always remain with you through the influence he has had on you and the part he has played in your lives.

The life we are contemplating was in many respects a sad and lonely one. By his own admission John was a bit of a wild boy in his younger days, and his poetry and writings indicate that he was a man who had loved and lost.

John was born in 1924. Not much is known about his early years but it's thought that he was placed in care when he was about two years old and spent most of his childhood away from his family.

Later he lived a transient lifestyle. He was living in a garage in Smith Road and working at a fish and chip shop in Unit Street in Country town when Mary first met him. He was being quite badly exploited and she found him some accommodation in Country town and they've remained friends ever since. George was popular wherever he went, a lot of people cared about him.

You'll smile as you think and talk about the things John did that endeared him to you. You'll think about what a worthwhile, decent and loving person he was. You'll remember how he loved to read the newspaper; he'd taught himself to read and write, and he'd read the newspaper from cover to cover It kept him in touch with the world.

That streak of independence stayed with John right to the end of his life. He was very much his own person and remained so even after his admission to Nursing Home. People soon learned to respect his personal space. He had his own names for all the nurses - not necessarily those that they called themselves, and he had his favourites,

He was a man of strong character; there was a frightening realness to him. True to those he trusted, loyal to those he believed in, he did not have an effortless life - the facts were not actively favourable to him. His had been a lonely existence, but he was compensated in the end by successive workers who appreciated his qualities, an adopted family of sorts who provided him with love and support in his last years. There are representatives here of most places George has stayed in the last few years.

Shakespeare said, in All's Well That Ends Well, "The web of our life is a mingled yarn of good and ill together: our virtues would be proud if our faults whipped them not; and our crimes would despair if they were not cherished by our own virtues."

Today we have the opportunity to say thank you to John for all the love he inspired in others. We say thank you to John

The Last Farewell

for the generosity of spirit he showed to others. We say thank you to John for his unique personality, for his ability to touch other people, to bring out the best in them, for being a really good friend.

To the end John was unique, he definitely marched to a different drum, he was proud and independent, he was endearing and loving, he never compromised, he never conformed. John was a real gentleman of the old school.

As we say our final goodbye to John I'd like to conclude our service with words of gratitude from Michael Leunig:

Gratitude from Michael Leunig read.

Tenderly and reverently, we say goodbye to our friend John, grateful for the life that has been lived; for all that life has meant to us. Here, in this last act, immune now to the changes and chances of this transient life, we entrust the body of John to its natural end, to its transformation into the ultimate elements of the universe.

We bid John farewell.

Funeral for a Difficult Person

Sometimes family relationships are strained, and the deceased may have been the cause of distress, either emotional or physical, for those in his life. People do not necessarily want to hide the pain that has been caused to them, simply because that person has died.

Such a ceremony needs to be crafted with sensitivity, and reflecting the needs of those who are left. Keep in mind that not all mourners will have had the same experience, resulting in division between the bereaved on the wording and conduct of the ceremony. As always, discuss the wording of the ceremony with the bereaved, and get the consent of the chief mourner before finalising the draft.

Potential wording

We have gathered to reflect on the life of Michael; and we have come for many reasons. Each person here has their own memories of Michael; some warm and happy memories and some that may cause pain. He was a human being, as are we all, and in his life journey he made mistakes as we all do. He led a life that was sometimes difficult for others to understand. Perhaps he couldn't always understand his own choices.

The challenge faced by those who are left behind is to choose to remember and hold within their hearts and minds those memories of Michael which bring happiness and a smile.

Other memories that bring pain need to be acknowledged and put to one side as you look to the future. Recalling them will not bring a sense of peace, nor will they change Michael's personal history. Held on to they could cause sadness and pain

The Last Farewell

to those who remain behind. Michael lived out many roles during his (relatively short) life: he was a son, a father, a partner, a neighbour, a colleague.

In each of those roles he sometimes succeeded, sometimes failed. We all do, to a lesser or greater extent. Michael had an influence on you and those around you. We do not easily choose to attend a ceremony such as this, and so your decision to come and honour the memory of Michael is appreciated by his family and those who loved him.

We join today to pay tribute, to celebrate and to honour the memory of a man who, at times, walked a different path. This final parting is bound to bring sorrow, whatever ties of love and friendship are involved. Today marks a final moment in our lives but it also marks the beginning of life as it will be without Michael.

The tide recedes but leaves behind bright seashells in the sand.
The sun goes down but gentle warmth still lingers on the land.
The music stops and
yet it echoes on in sweet refrains.
For every joy that passes
something beautiful remains
      M D Hughes

Interment of Ashes

Margaret Ann Davis

Much of what needed to be said about Margaret was voiced by many people at the ceremony we shared a few months ago. She touched so many as was evidenced on that occasion.

When the pain of grief eases, you will still feel that Margaret is all around you. She is in the garden she planned and planted, she is in her favourite chair, but importantly, she is in your hearts. She will feature frequently in your conversations as she is part of your living and shared memories.

No-one was prepared when Margaret left so suddenly. Ironically, Margaret was as she had meticulously planned for that day. It was a time of much sadness, but this is a time for peace. It is a time when we can lay her to rest and give thanks for the life that she lived and its influence on all of us.

She will not wish you to immerse yourselves in your grieving so that the world around you loses colour and is viewed in muted shades of grey. To grieve is wholly natural, and I know that you will miss her terribly, particularly at times when you least expect it, but Margaret is still with you and it is for each of you to learn to recognise the ways she is speaking and working in your lives on a daily basis. Be the people that Margaret loves, and live your lives as she would want you to.

Memories are wonderful things. They can be tender, loving and bittersweet. One thing you can be sure of is that they can never be taken away from you. Nothing can detract from the joy and the beauty of the memories you share with Margaret. Your love for her, and her love for you, can never be altered by time or circumstances. The memories are yours to keep. The past still travels with us, and what it has been makes us

The Last Farewell

what we are. Continue to grow as people and let her spirit abide with you always.

We don't say goodbye to Margaret, but lovingly and tenderly lay her Ashes to rest. We grieve at her death, but rejoice in the peace of knowing that nothing can ever part us.

May you all find comfort and richness in your hearts. May you find support and strength in your love for one another, and may you find peace.

> *As long as we can dream,*
> *as long as we can think*
> *as long as we have memory*
> *we will love you.*
> *As long as we have eyes to see*
> *and ears to hear and lips to speak ...*
> *we will love you.*
> *As long as we have*
> *a heart to feel ...*
> *a soul stirring within us,*
> *and imagination to hold you ... we will love you.*
> *As long as there is love*
> *and as long as we have breath to speak your name ...*
> *we will love you ... as you loved us*

Rest in Peace, Margaret.

Memorial Service

A memorial service is one at which no body is present, and may be held in days or weeks after the deceased has passed. A private funeral may already have been held by immediate family and close friends.

A memorial service may be held when a funeral is not feasible, (the deceased died in another location, or the body is not available) or perhaps it is a ceremony of recognition for a person of great public interest.

The structure of the ceremony is the same as for any other funeral, except that the deceased is not present.

The Last Farewell

Suicide

A funeral for someone who has died through suicide is always a sensitive issue, and the approach taken may vary according to the age of the deceased, though always in accordance with the wishes of the bereaved.

The question arises as to whether to mention the cause of the deceased's passing. Everyone will know, but the family may not want it to be talked about openly. Some people will have concerns based on religious beliefs that suicide is a sin. Others may want to highlight the mental health issues associated with this manner of choosing to die, raising the requirement for more funding services that can assist people who are experiencing life-threatening levels of distress. It is the celebrant's job to engage tact and not to cause additional distress in what is already an incredibly stressful situation, but to incorporate the issue in a compassionate manner.

If the person who has suicided is young, there is always a concern that one or more copycat deaths may follow. For that reason, the method of suicide is never disclosed.

In general, the ceremony will follow the format already discussed. The following passage references the reasons for this ceremony, and the impact that the death has had on everyone, with acknowledgement to Sue Hardy, fellow celebrant, for the words.

We meet today as a group of people whose lives have been abruptly changed by the death of one whom we deeply love. This change has brought mixed emotions for everyone, some confusion, anger, loneliness, fear, and longing. In the midst of these varied emotions, we long for peace and for endurance.

Everyone here today has somewhere else to be. Mary's death has brought us together under the most tragic of circumstances. As Mary's friend Peter said: "If she had died from an illness or accident, it would be much easier to accept that she is no longer with us."

Suicide leaves everyone with mixed emotions, a numbness, as we each search deep within our own souls trying to find answers, which just are not there. Often there is anguish over what might have been said or done that could have caused, or prevented, someone we know from feeling that the only possible solution to their feelings was to leave this world.

The Last Farewell

Pet Funerals

Taking steps to honour a pet and celebrate his or her important role in your life can help pet owners manage their grief. We love our animals so much, and it's so hard to let them go. The loss of any beloved pet has a drastic impact on our lives and is equal to or worse than that of losing a human family member. Losing a pet causes extreme anguish and sorrow. This is a natural reaction when you lose a loved one, whether human or animal; and the stages of mourning are the same. Grievers feel the identical shock and denial, anger and guilt, sorrow and depression.

Funeral ceremonies and rituals play an important part in meeting social and emotional needs, helping grieving pet owners to support one another as they come to terms with the reality of their loss.

To memorialise a pet is to acknowledge and honour the important role the pet played in the owners' life. It helps bring meaning to the loss and draw closure on grief.

It is particularly difficult for children to understand and come to terms with the loss of their pet animal, however, children thrive on ceremony and ritual and often enter into them with great enthusiasm. The joy discovered in 'celebrating the life of their pet' will ease the pain of the loss.

The pet has often been the last and closest companion for the elderly. This ceremony is the most difficult, as it is unlikely the elderly person will take on another animal. Great importance should be placed on honouring the passing of one so close.

Considerations for Paying Tribute to the Pet

- Select old snapshots for display
- Collect favourite playthings
- For children: allow them to paint or draw pictures on a piece of cloth to wrap the body of the pet and encourage grieving children to draw pictures or write stories inspired by their memories of their lost pet.
- Wrap the body in a favourite blanket
- Involve the whole family in the planning.
- Write an article, an anecdote, a story, a poem, a song, a letter, an obituary or a eulogy for the pet.
- Write a farewell letter to the pet as a way of saying an in-depth, thorough good-bye.
- Share anecdotes and favourite stories about the pet.
- Decorate a candle and light it in memory of the cherished pet.
- If the pet was a champion, decorate a tree or wreath with the pet's ribbons or awards, or make a memorial shadow box or scrapbook.
- Save something that belonged to the pet (collar, tags, food and water dishes; bed or blanket; toys; a clipping of fur or baby teeth; a feather; a horseshoe, tail and mane hairs from a horse; the wool from a llama) and during the ceremony, place in a special box for memory.
- Plant a tree, bush, shrub, garden or flowerbed as a permanent growing memorial to the pet.
- Mark the site with a memorial plaque, marker or statue.
- Use rituals or symbols to add meaning to the pet's farewell.
- Use rose petals or potpourri to create a sacred space.

The Last Farewell

- Encourage poetry and soft music to enhance the ceremony.

A ceremony for a pet is usually shorter than a funeral ceremony for a person. Children can be encouraged to speak, and this may assist in their grieving process. Various readings are suitable for a pet funeral and many will be located with a simple internet search.

The wording is as simple and varied as you would like to make it.

"We gather today to honour the memory of our special friend Rover, who spent his life in giving us so much joy and friendship; who expressed unconditional love and loyalty for the ten years in our company."

Rainbow Bridge

Just this side of heaven is a place called Rainbow Bridge. When an animal dies that has been especially close to someone here, that pet goes to Rainbow Bridge. There are meadows and hills for all our special friends so they can run and play together. There is plenty of food, water, and sunshine and our friends are warm and comfortable.

All the animals who have been ill or injured and old are restored to health and vigour; those who were hurt or maimed are made whole and strong again, just as we remember them in our dreams of days and times gone by. The animals are happy and content, except for one small thing; they each miss someone very special to them, who had to be left behind. They all run and play together, but the day comes when one suddenly stops and looks into the distance. His bright eyes are intent; his eager body begins to quiver. Suddenly, he begins to run from the group, flying over the green grass, his legs carrying him faster and faster.

You have been spotted, and when you and your special friend finally meet, you cling together in joyous reunion, never to be parted again. The happy kisses rain upon your face; your hands again caress the beloved head, and you look once more into the trusting eyes of your pet, so long gone from your life but never absent from your heart.

Then you cross over Rainbow Bridge together...
Anonymous

Let us now say our final farewell to Rover our dear and faithful companion. We place this (plant/stone/symbol) above his/her resting place so that when visiting this place we will remember her vitality, the fun times we shared and the love and trust she placed in us. Rest peacefully dear …

This is not a goodbye but a thank you. Thank you, Rover for touching our lives, for your loyalty and your love. Thank you for all the memories, for the fun of playing together, for the companionship. We will always remember the time you shared with us. Go safely now into your peaceful home in the sky. May there always be a bone for you to chew. We leave you now with our fond farewell.

Special Interest Funerals

At times you may be asked to preside over funerals that incorporate aspects of other religions, cultural beliefs, or interests. Friends and family will be your first source of information in respect of what is required, but otherwise you will need to undertake research, either via the internet, or through researching published material.

On one occasion, I presided over the civil funeral for a woman who had converted to Islam. The ceremony was held at a mosque, and the first portion was presided over by the Imam. I presided over the second portion in a room adjacent to the mosque for the benefit of her non-Muslim family and colleagues. There were some adjustments to be made in accommodating the needs of all parties, not just by myself but the mourners also.

Other ceremonies that may require research:
- Buddhist influenced ceremony
- New Orleans Jazz ceremony
- Ceremonies with Indigenous influences
- Ceremonies with cultural or ethnic influences

Music for a Funeral or Memorial Service

The inclusion of music within a ceremony is a matter of choice. There are many pieces of music that can be used, and often a piece is chosen which was a known favourite of the deceased. The following list provides some suggestions, although there are many other examples which may be suitable. Your celebrant or the funeral director may have some of these, but otherwise copies will have to be obtained.

Artist	*Song*
	Ave Maria
	As time goes by.
	Spirit in the Sky
Aled Jones	*Pie Jesu*
Aled Jones	*At the end of the day*
Andre Bocelli	*Time to say goodbye*
Andrew Lloyd Weber	*Amigos*
Andrew Lloyd Weber	*Memory*
Barbara Streisand	*The Way we were*
Bonnie Rait	*Feels like home*
Celine Dion	*My heart will go on*
Cinderella	*Stay in my arms*
Cleo Lane	*A time for Farewell*
Dire Straits	*So far away*
Dolly Parton	*I will always love you*
Elton John	*Song for Guy*
Eric Clapton	*Tears in Heaven*
Fiddler's Festival	*Ashokan Farewell*
Fleetwood Mac	*As long as you follow*
Graeme Connors	*A Sacred Place*
Hootie and the Blowfish	*Let her cry*

The Last Farewell

John Farnham	*You'll never walk alone*
John Farnham	*Angels*
John McNally	*Amazing Grace*
John Williams	*Cavatina*
Leonard Cohen	*Perfect Day*
Linda Ronstadt	*Goodbye my friend*
Linda Ronstadt	*I love you for sentimental reasons*
Mariah Carey	*Hero*
Mariah Carey	*One Sweet Day*
Matt Monro	*Softly as I leave You*
Nana Mouskouri	*Amazing Grace - track 21*
Nat King Cole	*Unforgettable*
Notting Hill Soundtrack	*When you say nothing at all*
Phil Collins	*Groovy Kind of Love*
Puff Daddy	*I'll be missing you*
REM	*Everybody Hurts*
Righteous Brothers	*Unchained Melody*
Sean Connery	*In My Life*
Shania Twain	*You're still the one.*
The Angels	*Be with you*
The Angels	*Be with you*
The Fureys	*The Old Man*
The Three Tenors	*Nessun Dorma*
The Three Tenors	*Amor, Vida De Mi Vidi*
The Verve	*Drugs don't work*
Tina Turner	*Simply the Best*
Vera Lynn	*We'll meet again*

Poems and Readings

There are many readings that may be suitable at the ceremony. Either the celebrant can read the chosen piece, or perhaps a friend or member of the family may like to contribute to the service in this manner. A small selection of poems is offered here, but others may be located with an internet search.

> I am standing upon the seashore. A ship at my side spreads her white sails to the morning breeze and starts for the blue ocean. She is an object of beauty and strength, and I stand and watch until at last she lands like a speck of white cloud just where the sea and sky come down to mingle with each other. Then someone at my side says, "There she goes!"
>
> Gone where? Gone from my sight ... that is all. She is just as large in mast and hull and spar as she was when she left my side and just as able to bear her load of living freight to the place of destination. Her diminished size is in me, not in her. And just at the moment when someone at my side says, "There she goes!" there are other eyes watching her coming and other voices ready to take up the glad shout, "Here she comes!"
>
> Henry Van Dyke.

The Last Farewell

Look to this Day
Look to this day,
For it is life, the very life of life.
In its brief course lie all the
Varieties and realities of your existence:
The bliss of growth,
The glory of action,
The splendour of beauty;
For yesterday is but a dream
And tomorrow is only a vision,
But to-day well lived makes
Every yesterday a dream of happiness,
And every to-morrow a vision of hope.
Look well therefore to this day!
Such is the salutation of the dawn.
   From the Sanskrit

Beyond
It seemeth such a little way to me
Across that strange country - the beyond
And yet not strange, for it has grown to be
The name of those whom I am most fond;
The make it seem familiar and most dear,
As journeying friends bring distant regions near,
And so to me there is no sting to death,
And so the grave has lost its victory
It is but crossing, - with abated breath
And white set face, - a little strip of sea
To find the loved ones waiting on the shore,
More beautiful more precious than before.
   Ella Wheeler Wilcox

Remember

Remember me when I am gone away,
Gone far away into the silent land;
When you can no more hold me by the hand,
Nor I half turn to go yet turning stay.
Remember me when no more day by day
You tell me of our future that you planned:
Only remember me; you understand
It will be too late to counsel then or pray.
Yet if you should forget me for a while
And afterwards remember, do not grieve:
For if the darkness and corruption leave
A vestige of the thoughts that once I had,
Better by far you should forget and smile
Than that you should remember and be sad.
   Christina Rossetti

I Did Not Die

Do not stand at my grave and weep
I am not there, I do not sleep.
I am a thousand winds that blow
I am the diamond glints on snow,
I am the sunlit ripened grain
I am the gentle autumn's rain.
When you awake in the morning hush
I am the swift, uplifting rush;
Of quiet birds in circled flight
I am the stars that shine at night
Do not stand at my grave and cry
I am not there. I did not die.
   Mary Elizabeth Frye

The Last Farewell

Death
You would know the secret of death.
But how shall you find it unless you seek it in the heart of life?
The owl whose night-bound eyes are blind unto the day
cannot unveil the mystery of light.
If you would indeed behold the spirit of death,
open your heart wide unto the body of life.
For life and death are one, even as the river and the sea are one.

In the depth of your hopes and desires lies your silent knowledge of the beyond;
And like seeds dreaming beneath the snow your heart dreams of spring.
Trust the dreams, for in them in hidden the gate to eternity.

Your fear of death is but the trembling of the shepherd
when he stands before the king whose hand is to be laid upon him in honour.
Is the shepherd not joyful beneath his trembling,
that he shall wear the mark of the king?
Yet is he not more mindful of his trembling?

For what is it to die but to stand naked in the wind and to melt into the sun?
And what is it to cease breathing, but to free the breath from its restless tides,
that it may rise and expand and seek God unencumbered?

Only when you drink from the river of silence shall you indeed sing.

And when you have reached the mountain top, then you shall begin to climb.
And when the earth shall claim your limbs, then you shall truly dance.

    - an extract from *The Prophet* by Kahlil Gibran.

Life Unbroken.
Death is nothing at all...
I have only slipped away into the next room.
I am I, and you are you...
Whatever we were to each other,
That we are still.
Call me by my old familiar name,
Speak to me in the easy way which you always used to.
Put no difference into your tone.
Wear no forced air of solemnity or sorrow.
Laugh as we always laughed at the little jokes we enjoyed together.
Play, smile, think of me, pray for me.
Let my name be ever the household word that it always was.
Let it be spoken without effort, without the ghost of a shadow on it.
Life means all that it has ever meant.
It is the same as it ever was;
There is absolutely unbroken continuity.
Why should I be out of mind because I am out of sight?
I am waiting for you for an interval,
Somewhere very near, just around the corner.
All is well.

    Henry-Scott Holland

The Dawn Service

A crisp, cold April morning, saw us gathered in the dark,
All around the massive shrine, there nestled in the park,
To give our thanks and our remembrance, to all those not returned,
From wars where so much blood had seen our nation's freedom earned.

And although we were a crowd, we were each a separate being,
Each a different, special scene, in our mind's eye we were seeing,
As the rifles fired and the bugle blew, 1 closed my eyes to stare,
At all the brave departed souls, that had proudly gathered there.

My beloved son beside me, and Dad's spirit too was there,
We three stood, and watched the dawn, in a silent wordless prayer,
I salute you, my country's sons, courageous, bold, and brave,
And know my woes are nothing, compared to what you gave.

Graeme Cook

A Grandmother's Mystery

What is it about a grandmother that is such a special bond,
Seeing not the years between us, but so very much beyond,
For being so much older, just doesn't seem to be the case,
The ages seem to melt to nought, within our own special place.
The place where we share our secrets, and it always just makes sense,
here my soul can be wide open, true and free without defence,
For being so much older, simply makes us both so nearer,
To words so true from both, whether you're the speaker or the hearer.
That very place where children sit, in safety and in pleasure,
To bask in love and comfort, is truly a child's life treasure.
Where a child can feel so grown up, and a Gran feel like a kid,
Learn and laugh from stories, of all the things she did.
The parents in the middle though, can't share this special caring,
It's just for us, my Gran and I, adventures we are sharing,
And even if my situation's bad, my Gran is not deterred,
What is it about a grandmother? I think Love, must be the word.

Graeme Cook

The Last Farewell

To Ride
Caring little for the elements, or the bugs that strikes my teeth,
Not just transportation, it's my passion there beneath,
Man and machine in oneness, as the scenes beside me gliding,
Not a lot can touch it, the pure pleasure of me riding.
Excitement, sure, exhilaration, always follows that white line,
But to tell the folk that just don't know, is impossible to define,
Luxury can be cold and stark, for a limousine I have no care,
Just that thrumming bike beneath me, and my head is in the air.
Graeme Cook

Crossing the Bar
Sunset and evening star
and one clear call for me!
And may there be no moaning of the bar
when 1 put out to sea.
But such a tide as moving seems asleep
to full for sound and foam
when that which drew them out the boundless deep
Turns again home.
Twilight and evening bell,
and after that the dark.
And may there be no sadness of farewell
when 1 embark.
For tho' from out our bourne of time and place,
the flood may bear me far
1 hope to see my pilot face to face
When 1 have crossed the bar.
Alfred, Lord Tennyson

Let me Go
When I come to the end of the road
and the sun has set for me
1 want no rites in a gloom filled room
Why cry for a soul set free?

Miss me a little, but not too long
and not with your head bowed low
Remember the love that we once shared
Miss me but let me go.

For this is a journey that we all must take
and each must go alone.
It's all a part of the Master's plan
a step on the road to home.

When you are lonely and sick at heart
Go to the friends we know
and bury your sorrows in doing good deeds.
Miss me, but let me go.
Christina Rossetti

The Last Farewell

Sympathy
There should be no despair for you
While nightly stars are burning,
While evening sheds its silent dew
Or sunshine gilds the morning.
There should be no despair, though tears
May flow down like a river:
Are not the best beloved of years
Around your heart forever?

They weep - you weep - it must be so;
Winds sigh as you are sighing;
And Winter ours its grief in snow
Where Autumn leaves are lying.
Yet they revive, and from their fate
Your fate cannot be parted
Then journey onward, not elated
But never broken-hearted.
Emily Bronte

The tide recedes, but leaves behind
bright seashells on the sand.
The sun goes down but gentle warmth
still lingers on the land.
The music stops and yet it lingers on
in sweet refrain.
For every joy that passes
something beautiful remains.
MD Hughes

Fisherman's Prayer
God grant that I may live
to fish until my dying day
And when it comes to my last cast,
I then most humbly pray
When In the Lord's safe landing net
I'm peacefully asleep -
That in His mercy I be judged
As good enough to keep.
Anonymous

Prayer by St Francis of Assisi
Lord,
Help me to live this day,
quietly, easily;
to lean upon your great strength,
trustfully, restfully;
to wait for the unfolding of your will,
patiently, serenely;
to meet others
peacefully, joyously;
To face tomorrow
Confidently, courageously.
Amen.

The Last Farewell

Check list of who to advise

This is not an exclusive list, but it is indicative or those people or organisations that must be notified in the event of a death.

The deceased person's doctor.
Family members, relatives and friends
Police in the absence of a doctor who could issue a certificate.
Funeral Director
Employer
Executor of the Will (where applicable)
Bank or Financial Institutions
Solicitor
Union
Professional Associations and Institutes
Clubs (e.g. RSL, Masonic, Rotary, Lions, Sporting, Social, Specific Interest, etc.)
Taxation Department
Department of Social Security
Department of Veterans Affairs
Insurance Company (Life, House, Car, Health, etc.)
Superannuation Company.
Health Fund
Electoral Office
Library - return any outstanding books
State Electricity Commission
Gas and Fuel Company
Internet Provider
Telecom
Cancel newspaper, milk and other deliveries (if appropriate)
Re-direct mail (if appropriate)
Cancel regular debits against the credit card or bank account.

You will also need to review the deceased's social media accounts, and close those. Hopefully, you have access to passwords, and can access their mobile phone if that is used for two-factor identification.

As a side note, password detail should be stored safely with the will for the benefit of the executor. Note that some accounts cannot be closed without the death certificate being provided.

Further Reading

Collins, Nigel **"Seasons of Life"**, 2000, Rationalist Press Ltd.

Moore, Faith**, "Celebrating a Life"**, 2009, Stewart Tabori & Chang, New York, USA

Seaburg, Carl **"Great Occasions**: Readings for the Celebration of Birth, Coming-of-Age, Marriage, and Death" 2003, Skinner House Books, Boston, USA

Searl, Edward "Beyond Absence". 2006, Skinner House Books, Boston, USA

It's Your funeral

A guide to planning your own funeral for when the time comes.

Rites of Passage
DOROTHY SHORNE

It's Your Funeral...

A guide to planning your funeral Ceremony

Dorothy Shorne

No part of this publication may be reproduced without prior written permission of the publisher. Ceremonies may be replicated for individual or celebrant use.

Note that Australian English is used in this book, and will vary in places to spelling used in the United States. Some terminology may be unfamiliar to readers outside of Australia.

Recognition is given to the
sharing of ideas and concepts
by fellow celebrants.

Printed April 2025
Copyright © Dorothy Shorne
ISBN: 978-1-7640472-0-3

Cover Image: DepositPhotos
Cover Design: Winsome Books

Winsome Books
Adelaide, South Australia

Contents

Introduction: Taking Charge of Your last Big Event 76
Chapter 1: Your Vision, Your Way 78
   1.1 How Do You Want to Be Remembered? 78
   1.2 Making it Personal 78
   1.3 Thinking Outside the Box 79
   1.4 The Guest List 82
Chapter 2: Deciding the Details 84
   2.1 Funeral Professionals 84
   2.2 Burial, Cremation, or Something Else? 85
   2.3 Venues 90
   2.4 Music: From Hymns to Your Favorite Rock Ballads 95
   2.5 Speakers and Stories: Who Will Take the Mic? 101
   2.6 Rituals, Traditions, and Ceremonial Elements 102
Chapter 3: Writing Your Own Eulogy 108
   3.1 Telling Your Story 108
   3.2 Adding a Touch of Humour (Because Why Not?) .. 110
   3.3 Amusing Epitaphs 111
   3.4 Famous Last Words 113
Chapter 4: Financial Considerations 115
Chapter 5: Navigating Legalities and Paperwork 118
   5.1 Wills, Executors, and Legalities 118
   5.2 Choosing an Executor 118
   5.3 Advance Directives and Living Wills: 120
   5.4 Informing Relevant Parties 121
   5.5 Organ Donation: Your Last Gift to the World 121
Chapter 6: Leaving a Legacy 123
   6.1 Personal Letters and Messages to Loved Ones 123
   6.2 Digital Legacies: Social Media, Passwords, and Online Memorials 124
   6.3 Creating a Lasting Impact 124
Chapter 7: When the Time Comes 126
Epilogue – perhaps for you the epitaph 128
About the Author 127
Also by Dorothy Shorne 128

Introduction: Taking Charge of Your last Big Event

We've all heard the comment that the only two sure things in life are death and taxes. I don't have much to say about taxes, except pay your fair share. Death is something that comes to us all. Sometimes it catches us unawares, and sometimes we are forewarned. In that case, we can have a say in the planning of what sort of funeral, celebration of life, or wake that we might like to have. It is the last opportunity to exert a level of control over an event in which our participation is limited.

Nobody wants to think about their own funeral. But it's going to happen at some point, and when it does, wouldn't it be reassuring to have it reflect exactly who you are? Planning your funeral may feel morbid at first, but think of it as organizing your final, unforgettable event—one that showcases your personality, values, and sense of humour (yes, even then!).

We plan birthday parties, weddings, and even retirement celebrations well in advance—events that celebrate life milestones. Why should your final farewell be any different? In fact, taking the time to plan your funeral isn't just about you (though it should reflect *you*); it's also one of the most caring things you can do for those you leave behind.

Without your guidance, your loved ones may be left guessing about what you'd have wanted—and during an emotional time, that can be tough. Planning your funeral is really just taking charge of your final curtain call, sparing your family a lot of uncertainty, and making sure your unique spirit shines through, even when you're not around to do the planning yourself.

You can contribute as much or as little as you like towards the event. You might just scan and compile a carousel of photographs; you might make notes that can be used by someone else writing your eulogy; you might leave information regarding the music and readings you would like; or you might just leave a substantial sum so that those left behind can give you're a great send-off at the wake.

On the other hand, you may like to take control of all of the above. Your funeral, your choice. By taking control of these details now, you'll not only spare your loved ones from guesswork and difficult decisions, but you'll also ensure that your send-off is done your way. Whether you want something simple, a celebration of life, or a mix of both, this guide will help you plan a farewell that's uniquely yours—perhaps with a few laughs along the way.

Chapter 1: Your Vision, Your Way

1.1 How Do You Want to Be Remembered?

Think about your life and how you want to be remembered. Are you someone who loved family gatherings, outdoor adventures, or quiet reflection? This section helps you consider the overall tone and message you want your funeral to convey.

Whether it's incorporating religious customs, cultural traditions, or quirky personal themes, the following suggestions emphasise aligning the service with personal values and life philosophies.

1.2 Making it Personal

You may prefer a quiet reflective service, or a celebration of life filled with stories and laughter might be more your style. Striking a balance between formal and light-hearted may help all concerned in honouring grief, while creating moments for honour, joy, and connection.

If you opt for a religious ceremony, the practices of that particular religion and the funeral conventions will strongly influence the ceremony that you may have. Meeting with the relevant religious officiant will give you guidance on the structure within which you may plan. Interfaith celebrants, or those who operate outside the confines of a regular church may be more flexible in their approach, and happy to work with you in devising a plan that suits you both.

You can choose readings, music, and nominate participants for your ceremony. Perhaps there are meaningful quotes you can use, which will have relevance and meaning for those who know you well. Infusing your personality into the ceremony will make it more significant for those who attend. Mourners often leave a funeral saying that they learned things about the deceased that they hadn't known before. This is your opportunity to tell friends and family the things they never knew about you, or the things you wish they had known.

You can tell people about your interests and hobbies, whether you loved gardening, sailing, or a good cup of coffee. Was social justice important to you? Did you campaign on different social issues? This is your sounding board, and unless you have written and published texts of various sorts, it is your last opportunity to express your opinions on the issues of importance to you.

This information doesn't have to be in the written form, though it may be. You can also record a video and tell your story in your own way. These days, most funeral companies and other venues have audio-visual facilities, so your video can easily be played on the day.

Other people will have their own observations and memories of their time with you, and you can invite family and friends to share their own tributes during the event. That usually takes place informally at the wake, but may also be included within the ceremony.

1.3 Thinking Outside the Box

Funerals do not have to be conventional. In deciding the format or structure you prefer it is important that the Funeral Director you choose understands your wishes and is accommodating. Not all funeral directors are flexible, so ask friends for referrals, and take note of any funerals you have attended at which you were impressed with the professional service provided.

You can explore options relating to the type of coffin or casket you would like. My father drove a Kombi Van for many years, and the family organised a cardboard coffin that was screen-printed with a Kombi driving through the Australian countryside. I have seen another similar coffin screen-printed with beautiful roses.

If you want to involve family and friends in the coffin design, you can request a plain coffin, and invite others to paint designs or motifs of their choice on it. They might like to write a final message - their choice. Another option is using a wicker basket type coffin. If your funeral director doesn't handle them, you will find suppliers on line. Purchasing advance means that you have to find somewhere to store it. Otherwise research delivery options with a short time frame.

If you are choosing a burial, the next choice will be where? A plot will need to be purchased if that hasn't already happened. Are you choosing a local cemetery where friends and family can visit if they wish, or somewhere else that has relevance for you? Burials are more expensive than cremations. They involve the purchase of the plot, usually a lease for a defined number of years, permits from the local authority, and payment for cemetery workers.

People in rural areas can sometimes arrange for a burial to take place on a rural property. This will be subject to regional legislative requirements. You will need to make your own enquiries in relation to that option.

Most people request a cremation. It is more cost-effective, and avoids the cost of a plot, although ashes may also be interred in a cemetery. There are options available for disposal of ashes, i.e.

- Scattering at sea;
    - Being made into a paperweight;
    - Being made into an item of jewellery; and
    - scattered in a favourite garden or bush location.

Be aware that ashes are alkaline, and a concentration of ashes in one location may be detrimental to the soil condition. For this reason, scattering of ashes is forbidden in some public gardens.

Urns can be purchased from funeral directors or funeral equipment suppliers, or you could commission an urn from a local pottery. Think outside the box; there are a range of containers that may be available. If this option is chosen, you will need to rely on a person to take possession of the urn. Have the conversation with them, because in this era of decluttering, it may not be convenient to lug around your ashes forever.

It's okay to ask for what you want. It's your party after all. You don't have to worry about what others think. Be sure to leave detailed written instructions with everyone who needs to know—the funeral company and your trusted family and friends.

1.4 The Guest List

When someone dies, there may be a mad panic in trying to work out who to notify of funeral arrangements, and how to contact them. Notices can be placed in the local newspaper, but readership is not what it used to be. Your friends and colleagues may also be scattered around the country, or even the world.

Social media is an option. If a trusted family member has access to your social media accounts, a notice can be place on the relevant platforms. It would be really helpful for those who are tasked with organising the day if you leave a list of people who you would like to attend, with their contact details. There will be others who attend of course. Word of mouth spreads, and people from you past may surface and also make an appearance. It's a great opportunity for them to re-connect with others who they haven't seen for years. In part, that's what funerals are all about.

The guest list represents your relationships and connections throughout your life, be they family, friends, colleagues, or those with common interests. Bringing together the people who have played a meaningful role in your life will be significant, not only to you in the planning phase, but to those people on the day. Make sure that the people who matter most to you are included, or at least invited.

Ultimately, it is the bereaved's choice regarding who to invite. They should feel empowered to include individuals who they believe would contribute positively to the atmosphere of the gathering.

It's Your Funeral

Leave advice on potential family dynamics or relationships that might complicate the guest list. Provide some suggestions on how to navigate sensitive situations, such as estranged family members or past conflicts. If there are people who you very specifically do not want to attend. include that detail with your funeral instructions, preferably with the reasons for that exclusion.

If you are enthusiastic about recording who is in attendance. you can purchase a guest book, or design and print one yourself. Guest books are often supplied by the funeral director (at a cost).

Many people will not be able to attend, because of distance or other factors. Consider organising a streaming service. Most funeral directors will be able to do this, but even a smart phone can be used combined with appropriate sharing software.

Chapter 2: Deciding the Details

2.1 Funeral Professionals

Depending on the country or state in which you live, it can be possible for the bereaved to manage the entire funeral process themselves, from transporting the body from place of death, to arranging the funeral and either cremation or burial. This is a huge imposition on those left behind, so it is easier for all concerned to engage a funeral director to manage the process for you. Visit different funeral companies, ask about the services they provide, and choose the one who you feel will be the most accommodating.

Funeral directors offer a packaged service, including completing the necessary administrative paperwork, publishing notices in the regional newspaper, printing memorial cards, ordering flowers, liaising with the cemetery or crematorium, and possibly supplying a celebrant. They may have a funeral chapel in which the ceremony can be conducted, and if so, will usually have audio-visual facilities which will enable the service to be live-streamed, and a slideshow of photographs to be shown.

This eases the burden on the bereaved of making arrangements at a time of significant stress. Not all the services offered by the funeral director need to be selected. You may direct that flowers are picked from your garden, or even that there not be any flowers. You can prepare a collection of the music you would like, and also prepare the audio-visual display. Explore the options.

It's Your Funeral

You can also choose your own funeral celebrant. Should you want a religious ceremony, the choices will be limited, but there are interfaith celebrants who will deliver a religious ceremony that meets your needs. Many people choose to have a secular, or civil celebrant. You can interview celebrants and choose the person you feel will deliver the service you require. Discuss the format you require for the ceremony and leave a written copy with them of your instructions. Contact details for this person should be included with the funeral details that are left for your executor.

2.2 Burial, Cremation, or Something Else?

Traditionally, people choose to be either buried or cremated. That decision is based on cost, family tradition, and other cultural practices.

The following non-traditional options will not be available everywhere, but you can research them now and leave advice and instructions in your funeral documentation. Some of the options will be quite expensive, so be sure to explore all the associated costs. For instance, a burial at sea, or even scattering of ashes at sea may involve chartering a boat.

1. Green Burial (Natural Burial)

What It Is: A green burial involves being buried in a biodegradable coffin or shroud, with no embalming chemicals or non-biodegradable materials. The goal is to return the body to the earth in a natural way, without disrupting the ecosystem.

Why Choose It: This option appeals to those who want an eco-friendly, natural way of returning to the earth, allowing their body to decompose and nourish the environment.

2. Burial at Sea

What It Is: Burial at sea involves either placing a whole body (in a biodegradable casket or shroud) or cremated ashes into the ocean. Regulations vary by country, but in many places, it's legal with proper permits and environmental considerations.

Why Choose It: For those who love the ocean or have a special connection to the sea, this is a beautiful, natural option that aligns with their passion for water or marine life.

3. Alkaline Hydrolysis (Aquamation or Water Cremation)

What It Is: Alkaline hydrolysis is an eco-friendly cremation alternative. The body is placed in a solution of water and potassium hydroxide, which breaks it down, leaving only the bones, which are processed into ash. The remaining solution is sterile and can be safely disposed of.

Why Choose It: This method uses less energy than traditional cremation and emits no harmful greenhouse gases, making it an environmentally friendly alternative.

4. Human Composting (Recomposition or Natural Organic Reduction)

What It Is: Human composting is a relatively new option where the body is placed in a vessel with organic materials (like wood chips, straw, and alfalfa) and naturally decomposes into nutrient-rich soil over a few weeks. The resulting compost can be returned to the family or used to grow plants.

Why Choose It: This is ideal for those committed to sustainability and the environment, as it creates fertile soil that can be used to nourish trees, gardens, or natural areas.

5. Resomation (Freeze-Drying or Cryomation)

What It Is: In this process, the body is frozen using liquid nitrogen, which makes it brittle. The body is then gently shattered into small particles and returned to the soil or placed in an urn. This method is similar to cremation but without burning.

Why Choose It: This method is energy-efficient and environmentally friendly, with no harmful emissions or chemical treatments.

6. Space Burial

What It Is: A portion of your cremated ashes is sent into space, where they can either orbit Earth or be launched into deep space. Companies offer services that can launch a symbolic amount of ashes into space, with the remainder kept by family or scattered elsewhere.

Why Choose It: This option appeals to those with a fascination with space exploration or those who want an extraordinary, celestial send-off.

7. Memorial Reefs

What It Is: Cremated remains are mixed with environmentally safe concrete to form artificial reefs, which are placed in the ocean to create new habitats for marine life. These reefs contribute to marine conservation while serving as a lasting memorial.

Why Choose It: For ocean lovers or those concerned with the health of marine ecosystems, becoming part of a living, underwater memorial can be a fulfilling choice.

8. Mushroom Burial Suit

What It Is: The mushroom burial suit is a biodegradable suit infused with mushroom spores that help decompose the body and remove toxins. This process allows the body to return to the earth in a cleaner, more efficient way.

Why Choose It: For eco-conscious individuals, this is a simple, natural way to return to the soil, with the added benefit of mushrooms breaking down harmful toxins.

9. Sky Burial (Tibetan Tradition)

What It Is: A traditional Tibetan practice, sky burial involves leaving the body on a mountaintop to be consumed by birds of prey. It's seen as a final act of generosity, returning the body to nature. Probably not available unless one is resident of Tibet.

Why Choose It: While rare and specific to certain cultures, this option symbolizes giving back to the natural world, and for those with ties to the tradition, it can be a deeply spiritual act.

10. Eternal Reefs or Living Memorials

What It Is: This involves mixing cremated remains into materials like soil or concrete to create memorial items that live on. Eternal reefs (as mentioned earlier) are one example, but there are also companies that create "living urns" where ashes are placed with tree saplings, which can be planted to grow a tree in your memory.

Why Choose It: These methods appeal to people who want to leave behind a living legacy—whether it's helping marine ecosystems or growing a tree that thrives for generations.

11. Memorial Jewellery or Diamonds

What It Is: Cremated remains can be turned into keepsake jewellery, such as glass beads or even synthetic diamonds, created from carbon extracted from the ashes. These items can be passed down as heirlooms or worn by loved ones.

Why Choose It: This is a deeply personal way to keep a part of you with your loved ones, offering a tangible connection they can hold onto.

A balanced look at the emotional, environmental, and financial aspects of each option will help guide the decision. Some of these options will be very expensive (sent into space, anyone?) so if you choose one of these, you will need to research the technicalities and leave sufficient funds.

2.3 Venues

Religious establishments and funeral homes provide venues for funeral ceremonies, but there are many non-traditional venues where a funeral or memorial service can be held, each offering a unique setting that reflects the individual's personality, passions, or life experiences.

With each, research practical consideration, such as is it feasible to bring a coffin or casket to the site, i.e. are there stairs to navigate; is there parking available; are permits required; and is there protection for mourners from inclement weather.

Here's a list of creative, meaningful locations for those seeking a departure from the conventional funeral home or church setting:

1. Beaches or Waterfronts

- **Why Choose It**: For people who had a love of the sea or water, a beach or lakeside setting can offer a peaceful, natural backdrop for their farewell. The soothing sound of waves and wide-open skies create a serene environment for reflection.
- **Considerations**: Make sure to check for local regulations on public gatherings and scattering ashes, as well as weather conditions.

2. Parks, Forests, or Gardens

- **Why Choose It**: Nature lovers may find deep meaning in holding a funeral or memorial service in a park, forest, or botanical garden. Surrounded by trees, flowers, and wildlife, this type of venue creates a

calming, beautiful space for remembrance. Perhaps the location has particular significance for you.
- **Considerations**: Look for venues that allow permits for gatherings, and consider whether guests can easily access the location.

3. Private Homes or Gardens

- **Why Choose It**: A funeral at home offers a deeply personal and intimate setting. Holding the service in the home or garden of the deceased (or a close family member) allows for a relaxed, familiar environment where loved ones can grieve and celebrate without the formalities of traditional venues.
- **Considerations**: Home funerals may require logistical planning for guests, catering, or equipment rentals like chairs or canopies.

4. Museums or Art Galleries

- **Why Choose It**: For art lovers or those with a cultural connection to a specific place, hosting a funeral in a museum or art gallery creates a reflective and unique atmosphere. Guests can move around exhibits, and the setting can symbolize a celebration of beauty, creativity, and history.
- **Considerations**: Many museums and galleries allow private event rentals, but availability and cost will vary. The chosen space may also limit the size of the gathering.

5. Theatres or Performance Spaces

- **Why Choose It**: For those who had a love of the performing arts—whether they were performers,

musicians, or theatre attendees—a local theatre or concert hall could provide a stage for their final act. The acoustics can be ideal for playing music, giving speeches, or even including performances in their honour.
- **Considerations**: Renting performance spaces can be expensive, so be sure to discuss budget and seating arrangements with the venue.

6. Outdoor Adventure Venues

- **Why Choose It**: For adventurers and thrill-seekers, locations like mountain summits, hiking trails, or outdoor adventure centres (like climbing walls or ski lodges) may be a fitting tribute. Holding a service in such a location can create a sense of connection with the individual's adventurous spirit.
- **Considerations**: Accessibility and weather should be planned carefully. It may also be best for smaller gatherings due to the location's limitations.

7. Vineyards, Wineries, or Breweries

- **Why Choose It**: For wine or beer enthusiasts, a vineyard or brewery can provide a beautiful, relaxed setting with rustic charm. The event can include toasts in the person's honour, creating a celebration-like atmosphere that reflects their personality.
- **Considerations**: Be sure to arrange for private event space and catering with the venue. Depending on the location, there may be restrictions on the type of service allowed.

8. Community Halls or Historical Buildings

It's Your Funeral

- **Why Choose It**: For those with strong ties to their community or local history, a community hall or historical building could be a meaningful venue. These spaces are often linked to the individual's past, offering a nostalgic and significant connection to their life.
- **Considerations**: Community halls are usually affordable and accessible, but you'll need to arrange your own decorations, seating, and refreshments.

9. Farms or Rural Properties

- **Why Choose It**: For people who lived in rural areas or had a deep connection to farming, hosting a service on a farm or ranch provides a rustic, pastoral backdrop. Being in a natural, open environment can give the service a peaceful and earthy feel.
- **Considerations**: Weather and outdoor facilities are factors to plan around, and you'll need to arrange logistics for any equipment or seating.

10. Boats or Yachts

- **Why Choose It**: For those who loved sailing or being on the water, chartering a boat or yacht allows for a unique service. The funeral can take place as the boat moves along a river, lake, or ocean, creating an intimate and scenic farewell.
- **Considerations**: It's important to check local laws about holding services on boats or scattering ashes at sea, and consider whether guests are comfortable with being on the water.

11. Outdoor Event Spaces

- **Why Choose It**: Rustic barns or open-air event spaces are ideal for those who loved the countryside, outdoor living, or a more informal, nature-connected lifestyle. These spaces offer charm, privacy, and often beautiful views.
- **Considerations**: Many venues offer rentals for weddings and can easily adapt to funeral services, but availability may depend on season and event schedules.

12. Libraries or Bookstores

- **Why Choose It**: For avid readers or lifelong learners, a library or independent bookstore provides a cozy, intellectual setting. You can honour their love of literature, learning, or knowledge in a meaningful way by surrounding guests with their favourite books and authors.
- **Considerations**: Some libraries allow rentals for private events, but availability and rental policies will vary. It may be ideal for a smaller, more intimate service.

13. Zoos or Wildlife Reserves

- **Why Choose It**: For those with a passion for wildlife, nature conservation, or animals, holding a memorial at a zoo or wildlife reserve can be an extraordinary tribute. The setting can reflect their commitment to animal welfare or their deep connection to nature.
- **Considerations**: Some zoos and reserves offer event spaces, but they often have specific regulations, and costs can vary depending on the venue's policies.

14. Sports Venues or Stadiums

- **Why Choose It**: For sports fans or athletes, holding a funeral at a sports venue or stadium offers a grand and fitting farewell. Whether it's a football field, tennis court, or golf course, the venue can reflect their passion for the game.
- **Considerations**: You'll need to arrange with the venue and consider whether the atmosphere aligns with the tone you want to set. It's ideal for larger gatherings.

15. Campsites or National Parks

- **Why Choose It**: For outdoor enthusiasts, camping sites or national parks offer breathtaking, natural landscapes. Whether in a forest, by a lake, or under the stars, these locations reflect a love of adventure and connection to the wilderness.
- **Considerations**: You may need permits to gather in national parks or campsites, and plan for outdoor logistics, such as seating, weather, and transportation.

These non-traditional venues allow for personalization and can create an atmosphere that honours the individual in a memorable and meaningful way. They also offer flexibility, whether you're looking for something intimate or grand, serene or celebratory.

2.4 Music: From Hymns to Your Favorite Rock Ballads

Choosing the right music for a funeral can evoke memories, comfort attendees, and celebrate the life of the person being honoured. The music you select can reflect your personality, values, or favourite genres. You may like to hire musicians, have loved ones perform, or instead create a custom playlist to be played electronically.

Here are some suggestions across different styles and themes to help guide your choices.

1. Classical and Instrumental Music

- Classical pieces are timeless, serene, and can add an air of reverence or reflection to a service.

- **"Canon in D" by Johann Pachelbel**: A gentle, peaceful piece often used for moments of reflection.

- **"Air on the G String" by Johann Sebastian Bach**: Calm and soothing, perfect for a quiet, meditative atmosphere.

- **"Clair de Lune" by Claude Debussy**: A soft, emotional piano piece that conveys beauty and tenderness.

- **"Ave Maria" by Franz Schubert or Charles Gounod**: A traditional choice, often used for religious services or to bring comfort.

- **"Nimrod" from *Enigma Variations* by Edward Elgar**: A solemn and powerful orchestral piece often played at memorials.

2. Popular Songs (Classic and Modern)

- Popular songs can reflect the individual's taste in music or share messages of love, hope, and remembrance.

- **"Somewhere Over the Rainbow" by Israel Kamakawiwo'ole**: A beautiful, uplifting ukulele rendition, often associated with a sense of peace and optimism.

- **"What a Wonderful World" by Louis Armstrong**: A joyful, reflective song that celebrates the beauty of life.

- **"Imagine" by John Lennon**: A hopeful and reflective song with a message of peace and unity.

- **"Tears in Heaven" by Eric Clapton**: A deeply emotional song about loss and the hope of being reunited in the afterlife.

- **"Wind Beneath My Wings" by Bette Midler**: Often played at memorials, this song honors the support and love shared in life.

- **"My Way" by Frank Sinatra**: For someone who lived life on their own terms, this classic song can be a bold, fitting tribute.

3. Spiritual and Religious Hymns

- If the deceased had a spiritual or religious background, hymns can provide comfort and a connection to faith.

- **"Amazing Grace"**: A universally loved hymn about redemption and grace, often played on bagpipes or sung in services.

- **"The Lord's My Shepherd" (Psalm 23)**: A comforting hymn with a message of trust in God's protection and care.

- **"Abide with Me"**: A hymn often sung at memorials, offering solace and strength in times of difficulty.

- **"How Great Thou Art"**: A powerful, uplifting hymn that celebrates God's greatness.

- **"Ave Verum Corpus" by Wolfgang Amadeus Mozart**: A moving, spiritual piece often used in Catholic services.

4. Folk and Acoustic

- For a more intimate, personal feel, folk and acoustic songs can convey warmth, reflection, and a sense of closeness.

- **"The Parting Glass" (traditional Irish folk song)**: A reflective song about bidding farewell, often played at wakes or memorials.

- **"Blackbird" by The Beatles**: A simple acoustic song with themes of hope and new beginnings.

- **"Hallelujah" by Leonard Cohen (or versions by Jeff Buckley, k.d. lang)**: A hauntingly beautiful song about life's trials, love, and loss.

- **"I Will Remember You" by Sarah McLachlan**: A soft, emotional song that speaks of remembrance and farewell.

- **"You've Got a Friend" by Carole King**: A comforting song about lasting friendship and support.

5. Uplifting or Celebratory Songs

- For those who want a more positive, celebratory tone, uplifting songs can focus on joy, gratitude, and celebration of life.

- **"Don't Stop Me Now" by Queen**: A fun, upbeat song for someone with a larger-than-life personality who lived to the fullest.

- **"Always Look on the Bright Side of Life" by Monty Python**: A light-hearted, humorous option for those who appreciated a bit of irreverence and wit.

- **"Three Little Birds" by Bob Marley**: A positive, laid-back song with the message, "Every little thing is gonna be alright."

- **"Lean on Me" by Bill Withers**: An uplifting song about supporting one another through tough times.

- **"Here Comes the Sun" by The Beatles**: An optimistic song, perfect for honoring new beginnings and hope after dark times.

6. Movie or Television Soundtracks

- Iconic film scores or theme songs can be powerful, personal choices, especially if the deceased had a special connection to a particular movie or show.

- **"Time" by Hans Zimmer (from *Inception*)**: A deeply emotional, slow-building orchestral piece that evokes reflection.

- **"Theme from *Schindler's List*" by John Williams**: A hauntingly beautiful violin melody, filled with emotion and sorrow.

- **"The Circle of Life"** from *The Lion King*: For someone with a connection to nature or who embraced the idea of life's cyclical nature.
- **"Main Theme"** from *The Lord of the Rings* **by Howard Shore**: A majestic, sweeping score for fantasy lovers or those who appreciated epic storytelling.
- **"My Heart Will Go On" by Celine Dion (from** *Titanic*): An iconic song about everlasting love and remembrance.

7. Jazz and Blues
- For those who loved jazz or blues, these genres offer a range of deeply emotional, soothing, or even celebratory pieces.
- **"Ain't No Sunshine" by Bill Withers**: A soulful, poignant song about loss.
- **"What a Difference a Day Made" by Dinah Washington**: A soothing jazz classic with themes of love and transformation.
- **"Summertime" by Ella Fitzgerald**: A laid-back, classic jazz piece that evokes peace and warmth.
- **"Feeling Good" by Nina Simone**: A powerful song about personal freedom and renewal, for someone who embraced life with joy and intensity.

8. Contemporary and Indie Choices

It's Your Funeral

- If the deceased preferred more contemporary or indie music, here are some options with emotional depth and thoughtful lyrics.

- **"The Night We Met" by Lord Huron**: A moving, atmospheric song about longing and reflection.

- **"See You Again" by Wiz Khalifa ft. Charlie Puth**: A contemporary song about friendship, loss, and the hope of reuniting.

- **"Holocene" by Bon Iver**: A meditative, atmospheric song perfect for a quiet moment of reflection.

- **"Gone Away" by The Offspring**: A powerful rock ballad about loss and missing someone deeply.

- **"Saturn" by Sleeping at Last**: An ethereal, emotional song that deals with life, death, and the beauty of existence.

The music you choose can provide comfort, evoke memories, and set the tone for the type of farewell you envision. Whether you want something sombre, uplifting, reflective, or light-hearted, music helps create the emotional backdrop for saying goodbye.

2.5 Speakers and Stories: Who Will Take the Mic?

Who will speak at your funeral? Family or friends can be asked to deliver the eulogy, tributes, or readings. Some people will happily do so, but others will cringe at the thought of speaking in public. Choose those speakers with thought and care. They should prepare their tribute in advance, and read it aloud several times. Doing so helps to de-sensitise the emotion of the moment, so that they deliver their words during the ceremony without breaking down. If they do however, that is okay.

Ultimately, it is up to the bereaved what they say on the day, but you can leave behind guidance on the of stories or themes you'd like shared—whether you prefer heartfelt memories, humorous anecdotes, or a mix.

After the anticipated speakers have addressed the mourners, the celebrant can invite anyone else to speak, if this is appropriate. This extends the opportunity to share memories or special stories with everyone, but this may not be an option if there is a time restriction on the length of the ceremony. Restrictions are likely to apply if the ceremony is being held at a crematorium, or a funeral home.

2.6 Rituals, Traditions, and Ceremonial Elements

Symbolic gestures add depth and personal significance to your funeral, turning it from a simple ceremony into a meaningful tribute to your life, values, and connections with others. Whether rooted in cultural traditions or your own personal creativity, these gestures can be powerful ways to express who you are and leave a lasting memory for those attending. Here are some ideas to help you create those special moments.

Those gestures may be rooted in religious or cultural tradition, or may reflect your personal beliefs or connections. The following are some suggestions for creating moments of meaning:

Planting Trees or Flowers

- Living Memorials: Have guests plant trees, flowers, or saplings in your honour. This creates a living tribute that grows and flourishes, symbolizing your continued presence in the lives of your loved ones. It can be part of the funeral itself or done at a later memorial gathering.

- Creating a Legacy Garden: If you have a particular love for nature, why not have guests contribute to a communal garden or natural space? Each guest can plant a small seedling or flower, creating something beautiful and lasting in your memory.

Candle Lighting Ceremonies

- Light in the Darkness: Lighting candles can symbolize hope, remembrance, and love. You can incorporate a candle-lighting ceremony where each guest lights a candle in your honour, creating a warm, peaceful atmosphere. Some may light candles while sharing a memory or a wish for your peace.

- Passing the Flame: Another variation is passing a single flame from person to person, representing the connection and bond between family and friends. As each person lights their candle from yours, it symbolizes your impact on their lives.

Releasing Doves, or Butterflies

- Butterfly or Dove Release: For a more natural touch, releasing butterflies or doves at the end of the ceremony can represent the soul's journey, peace, and transformation. This is a particularly moving way to symbolize departure with beauty and grace. Keep in mind that the while the doves will fly back to their coup, the butterflies will likely die away from their natural environment and food source.

- Balloons or Lanterns: The symbolic release of balloons or sky lanterns can represent letting go, freedom, or sending a final message to you. This option is **not recommended**, because of resultant litter, and potential harm to wildlife who may ingest the balloons, or get tangled up in the strings. It will be forbidden in some locations.

Writing Letters or Messages

- Farewell Letters: Invite guests to write private letters to you, sharing memories, thanks, or their thoughts. These letters can be placed in your casket or an urn, creating a deeply personal farewell.

- Memory Jars or Boxes: Set up a memory jar or box where attendees can drop notes about favourite moments, how they will remember you, or words of comfort for your family. These can later be shared with loved ones as a way to continue connecting with your spirit.

Symbolic Items or Offerings

- Placing Objects in the Casket: Encourage loved ones to place meaningful items—letters, photos, or small personal objects—into your casket or next to your urn. These items may represent memories, shared experiences, or tokens of affection.

- Group Offerings: Similar to placing objects in a casket, you can have a symbolic group offering where guests lay flowers, stones, or other tokens on a central table or around your resting place, creating a collective tribute.

- Pouring a Toast: For a light-hearted gesture, guests could pour a small glass of your favourite drink—wine, whiskey, tea—and offer a final toast in your honour. This can be a warm and intimate moment, especially for informal or celebratory gatherings.

Creating a Time Capsule

- Preserving Memories for the Future: Consider organizing a time capsule where family and friends contribute items, notes, or photos. This could be buried at a special spot, perhaps near your grave or another meaningful place, to be opened on a significant future date, allowing loved ones to reflect and reconnect with your memory.

- Personalized Time Capsules: For a more personal twist, you could leave a time capsule behind for your loved ones, with letters, objects, or even a recorded message for them to discover on a future date, keeping your connection alive.

Rituals with Water, Sand, or Earth
- Water Ceremonies: If your life was closely tied to the sea or rivers, incorporating water into your service can be beautiful. Guests can pour water into a communal vessel, or take water from the ocean, a lake, or another body of water to scatter along with your ashes.

- Earth and Sand Rituals: Symbolic gestures like pouring sand or earth over your casket (or at a chosen spot) can represent returning to nature, grounding, and peace. This can be combined with cultural traditions or done informally, offering loved ones a tangible way to say goodbye.

Personal Touches in Farewell Rituals
- Passions and Hobbies: If you had a particular passion—like painting, music, or cooking—incorporate it as a symbolic gesture. For example, a musician may have a group play a song in tribute; a chef might ask friends to share a favourite recipe. These small gestures show that life's joy continues even in farewell.

- Symbolic Gifts for Guests: Offer guests a small memento tied to the symbolism of your life. It could be a personalized stone, a packet of seeds, or even a small notebook for recording memories. These keepsakes allow guests to take a piece of you with them, creating a tangible link. *At my mother's funeral, my sisters and I baked Chocolate Chip biscuits using her recipe. We packed them in small cellophane bags, and invited mourners to take a bag. The recipe was printed on the back of the memorial card.*

Symbolic gestures allow readers to express their individuality and create lasting, heartfelt memories that live on beyond the funeral itself. These meaningful acts, both simple and profound, can help loved ones find comfort and healing.

Chapter 3: Writing Your Own Eulogy

This is where the mourners will hear your voice and story, whether in written or spoken format. Being able to craft this is a key reason for planning your own funeral.

3.1 Telling Your Story

This is your opportunity to tell your story however you want. It can be written and left for a trusted person to read, you can make a voice recording, or you can make a video. Summing up a life well-lived may seem initially to be a daunting prospect, but working within a framework makes it easier. There is no right or wrong way to develop this presentation or address. It's your story after all.

You can break it into sections.

Opening Statement: Briefly introduce yourself and your essential life details.

Life Journey: Highlight significant milestones, such as education, career, and personal achievements, while maintaining authenticity.

Personal Touches: Include anecdotes that reveal your character, hobbies, passions, and interests, giving readers a glimpse into who you are.

Including Family and Relationships: Acknowledge loved ones in a way that honours their importance in your life without creating a lengthy list that detracts from the narrative.

Conveying Values and Beliefs: Share personal philosophies, values, and lessons learned throughout your life, giving insight into what mattered most to you.

It's Your Funeral

The following dot points serve as a guide to the issues that might be covered. They are not all-inclusive, and there may be additional anecdotes or memories that you would like to have included. It is not necessary that all of the dot points are covered – they are presented as suggestions only.

- Name
- Date of Birth
- Place of Birth
- Parents, Brothers and Sisters
- Early life and family, parent's occupation, early home life, childhood interests, areas in which the family lived.
- Education – Primary, Secondary, Tertiary
- Trade/Profession
- Courtship/Marriage
- Children and Family Life
- Places where family lived/work places
- Personality/ characteristics/ sense of humour
- Community Service
- Achievements
- Beliefs
- Causes
- Political Ideals
- Recreation/ Sports/ Hobbies
- Likes and dislikes – Music, the Arts, Poetry, Literature, Television, Radio
- Travel
- Animals
- Illness and cause of death
- Any other relevant information.

Conclusion

Writing your own eulogy is an opportunity to celebrate life, reflect on your accomplishments, and leave a lasting legacy for those who remain. While it is a serious task, incorporating humour and personal stories can create a beautiful and meaningful tribute that resonates with others. The eulogy is delivered during the ceremony, but the content is often used as the basis for an obituary, either in print or in an online forum.

3.2 Adding a Touch of Humour (Because Why Not?)

Funerals don't need to be morose affairs, though obviously there will be an element of sadness, grieving, and regret. While death is serious, and will leave many people feeling bereft, life is filled with moments of joy, laughter and absurdity. Humour can be a powerful tool for healing during times of grief, and can both help to lighten the emotional burden and also foster connection among the mourners.

Infusing Humour into the Planning Process

If you are involving others into the planning process, you can have light-hearted discussions when planning the details. This can create a supportive environment where everyone feels comfortable sharing their ideas.

Using this input, you can craft a eulogy that balances heartfelt sentiments with humour. You may like to include amusing stories, reflecting episodes of your life and interactions with others. Your nearest and dearest may like to tell their own stories when they speak during the ceremony, or else sharing them at the wake.

Respecting Boundaries

Know Your Audience. Be sensitive to the feelings of others. Not everyone may appreciate humour during such a complex time, so gauge the comfort level of those attending. Striking a Balance between humour and solemnity, ensuring that the humour feels respectful and appropriate within the context of the memorial.

Final Thoughts on Humour and Remembrance

Incorporating humour into epitaphs, last words, and other final flourishes can provide a light-hearted touch to memorials, reflecting the personality of the deceased while also offering a moment of levity during a difficult time. Here are some examples and ideas for funny epitaphs and last words:

3.3 Amusing Epitaphs

"I told you I was sick!"
A playful nod to the deceased's humour about their own mortality.

"Here lies [Name], who finally caught that elusive nap."
A light-hearted take on the universal desire for rest.

"Gone to join the circus."
A whimsical way to suggest that the deceased has embarked on a new adventure.

"I'm just resting my eyes."

A humorous statement implying that the deceased is merely taking a break.

"Don't worry, I'm not really gone; I'm just in another room."
A comforting thought for loved ones, adding a humorous twist.

"I may be dead, but I still have more followers than you."
A funny take on social media culture, perfect for a digitally savvy individual.

"Finally got that promotion to 'permanent vacation'!"
A humorous perspective on the afterlife.

"Rest in pieces!"
A cheeky twist on the traditional "rest in peace."

"I'm in a better place—at least I hope so!"
A light-hearted expression of hope regarding the afterlife.

Funny Last Words
"I guess this is the end of my 'thrilling adventure'!"
A humorous acknowledgment of the finality of life.

"If you're reading this, I'm not as good at hiding as I thought."
A funny take on the idea of "hiding" from life's troubles.

"Can someone tell the pizza guy I'm not home?"

A light-hearted comment about everyday life, perfect for a food lover.

"I can't believe I'm missing the next season of my favourite show!"
A humorous reference to the inevitability of life continuing without them.

"I'd like to thank my parents for bringing me into this world, and my kids for making me want to leave it!"
A playful jab at the trials of parenting.

3.4 Famous Last Words

Winston Churchill:
Though not necessarily humorous, Churchill's reported last words were, "I'm bored with it all," reflecting his characteristic wit and candour.

Thomas Edison:
Edison reportedly said, "It is very beautiful over there," shortly before he passed, showcasing a serene perspective on death.

Oscar Wilde:
Wilde's last words were humorously quoted as, "Either that wallpaper goes, or I do," a reflection of his sharp wit.

David Foster Wallace:
His last words were reportedly, "I just don't know how to be happy," which, while sombre, also encapsulate a humorous and self-aware view of his struggles.

Conclusion

While the funny epitaphs and last words shared earlier are not directly attributed to specific individuals, they draw inspiration from this rich tradition of humour surrounding death. Many modern humorous epitaphs are crafted by families, friends, or funeral planners to reflect the deceased's personality, creating a personalized tribute that often resonates with those who knew them.

A word of warning; trying to incorporate too many elements can overwhelm attendees and detract from the focus of the service.

Chapter 4: Financial Considerations

4.1 Budgeting for the Big Event

Expenses will vary widely, depending on location, type of service, and what services are included. They will also differ widely between different funeral directors, so you will need to do your research. Financial allowance will need to be made for:

- Basic service fees (funeral director and staff)
- Casket or urn costs
- Embalming and preparation
- Use of facilities for services (chapel, reception area)
- Transportation (hearse, limousines)
- Grave plot and burial fees (or cremation costs)
- Memorial items (programs, headstones)
- Additional services (music, flowers, catering)

Identify essential services versus optional extras. Think about what you or your family could provide that might reduce the costs, and also make the event more personalised. Can a clever friend design the memorial cards? Ask everyone to bring a bunch of flowers from their garden. Mourners might be happy to bring a plate of food for the wake, and perhaps that event can be held in a local community hall, a park, or someone's home. Explore the options.

Don't forget leaving funds for the wake. Do you want a simple event or a full-scale party? Will you lay on the champagne and caviar? Whatever, there will be some cost involved, ranging from facilities hire to food and drink.

If you are making financial provision for the event, funds need to be left where someone else can access them, with written advice on your plan and intentions.

4.2 Pre-Paying vs. Leaving the Bill to Someone Else

You can pre-pay the funeral director, covering much of the cost. That minimises the burden on those left behind, and simplifies organisation. By entering into a contract with the company, you can be sure that your wishes will be honoured.

If this option is chosen, there is a minimal risk that the company will go out of business, and your funds will be lost. Flexibility is also lost if for some reason, circumstances change at a later date, such as moving location, or changing preferences. It may restrict the mourners from holding the ceremony that would meet their needs.

You will need to weigh up these issues in making this decision

4.3 Leaving the Bill to Loved Ones

The other option is to leave funds in your estate, or to assume that the bereaved will be able to pay. If you are leaving funds, they need to be accessible at short notice. If you haven't budgeted correctly, that shortfall will need to be made up from elsewhere—presumably your friends and family. They may be in a position to do this, but if not, they may have to curtail the funeral you have planned. It can also lead to family disputes about the sharing of costs and the choices and subsequent expenses relating to the funeral.

There is no right or wrong option here. You will know your circumstances and what is a reasonable path to take in relation to finances. In the spirit of openness, you could also discuss these issues with your family, or those on whom will fall the task of implanting your wishes.

A pre-paid insurance bond specifically to address the cost of a funeral may be an option.

4.4 Affordable Alternatives and Creative Cost-Cutting

If affording the cost remains a consideration, there are some alternatives to traditional funerals, such as requesting a direct cremation or burial, and bypassing the funeral service. A memorial or celebration of life event can still be held in a public place or even a private home. Green burials or eco-friendly options may be less expensive.

As mentioned previously, there are cost saving options with creating personalised memorial programs, presenting photo displays, and providing musicians. Online platforms can be used for invitations and announcements to save on printing costs.

Conclusion

With effective planning and research in advance, you can make informed decisions about the costs associated with your funeral plan. Being proactive about financial considerations can reduce stress and ensure that the final wishes are honoured without placing an undue burden on loved ones. Sensible also is to discuss your financial plans and wishes openly with family members so they are familiar with your expectations when the time comes.

Chapter 5: Navigating Legalities and Paperwork

5.1 Wills, Executors, and Legalities

This topic strays from funeral planning, but it is associated and it is definitely important. Leaving a professionally drafted will is life planning. A will outlines your wishes regarding the distribution of assets, care of dependents, and funeral arrangements. It stipulates any bequests that you want, and ensures clarity at a time of stress and emotion.

There are will kits available in most countries, but in general, the cost of engaging a solicitor to record your wishes in a document that is legally enforceable is worth it. Legislation regarding the requirements for an enforceable will differs in different jurisdictions, and a generic will kit might not meet those requirements. In that case, the will could be challenged, and the subsequent costs are usually taken from the estate. There may not be anything left to distribute in that situation.

5.2 Choosing an Executor

You must appoint an executor within your will. This is the person, or persons, who will manage your estate and will ensure that your wishes are carried out as specified in the will. They will handle financial and legal affairs, including settling debts and distributing assets. Typically, this is the person who liaises with the funeral home and other service providers.

The role of executor can be quite involved and time-consuming. You should consider carefully who you appoint to this role, and be sure that they are both capable and willing to undertake the task. You may appoint two or even more people to be executors of your will, and in that case, you need to decide if all decisions can be made severally, or must be made together.

You may decide to appoint at least two executors if there are concerns that one of them might not be available when the times comes. Perhaps one of them will be travelling, or otherwise unavailable. It is also a good idea to review your will on a regular basis, and to ensure that the executors initially appointed are still appropriate and available.

Don't assume that the executor will know and understand your wishes in relation to disposal of your estate and provision for your dependants. You should outline that in writing, but sit down with them in advance and have the conversation. Pour them a drink and explain what you want and what it means to you.

If you have children who have not yet reached the age of majority, you will need to appoint guardians for them. The executor may fulfill that role, but not necessarily. Guardianship is an important responsibility, and you need to be sure that the person(s) you appoint are willing to take on that role, and also has the capacity to do so. They will need to understand your values and the type of upbringing you want for your children. They will also require access to adequate finance to carry out those wishes. Discuss with your financial adviser whether a trust should be put in place for that purpose. Although legal requirements for creating a valid will vary according to the local legislature, there are some factors in common.

- A person must be of required age;
- A person must be of sound mind;
- A person must be deemed competent
- There should not be duress or coercion involved; and

- The will should be witnessed. Those witnesses should not also be beneficiaries.

5.3 Advance Directives and Living Wills:

The process of dying is not always a simple affair. You may undergo a period of illness and incapacitation. In that situation, you need someone who can advocate for you in varying areas of your life: in relation to your finances, managing your assets, and ensuring your wishes in regard to medical treatment are communicated to the relevant professionals.

Documentation should be prepared at the same time as your will that covers these requirements. Those documents will vary, according to where you live and the relevant legislation, but will likely be:

- Power of Attorney. This document will grant another person to administer your financial affairs on your behalf. If this person also has the ability to transact in property on your behalf, the Power of Attorney may have to be lodged with the relevant land registration authority. Consult a solicitor for advice in this regard at the time of signing the document.
- Advanced Care Directive. This document stipulates your wishes in relation to decisions to be made on your behalf, should you not be in a position to communicate them at that time. It also stipulates who has the authority to act on those decisions. It also advises your medical carers on the treatment you require, or at what time, treatment should desist
- Living Will. Similar to the Advanced Care Directive. It informs your medical practitioners or your wishes

It's Your Funeral

in relation to your preferences for medical treatment if you are unable to make those decisions for yourself.

5.4 Informing Relevant Parties

Again, as previous mentioned in relation to critical documentation, your executor, family, and any appointed agents should be advised or your wishes to ensure they are known and respected. The documents that you prepare should be updated periodically to cover any changing circumstances. It is critical that the persons who are given authority under these documents fully understand your intentions, and can be trusted to act accordingly.

5.5 Organ Donation: Your Last Gift to the World

Have you considered organ donation? It is not possible in all cases, such as when a person has particular illnesses, or has had specific treatments, but in the case of accidental death, assuming that a person has indicated a prior intention to do so, some organs can be donated to someone else in need. This has potential impact on saving lives.

In the state in which I live, agreement to be an organ donor is indicated on a driver's licence. Next of kin can over-ride that decision, so it is important to have the conversation outlining your philosophy on organ donation and intention to do so, if the circumstances arise.

Living donations are possible, such as kidney or bone marrow transplants, but in this instance, I am referring to donations in the event of your untimely demise. Your intentions can be documented in your will or advanced care directive, with that decision made known to your executors and close family members.

Be assured that medical professionals follow strict guidelines to ensure that the dignity and care of a deceased person are upheld, and there are strict procedures surrounding the quality of care received in final days, hours or moments of life, and the steps taken in declaration of death.

Conclusion

Being proactive about legal considerations can provide peace of mind, knowing that your preferences will be honoured and respected. Maintaining dialogue with those who are left to implement your wishes ensures that your intentions and wishes remain clear, and your preferences should be honoured and respected.

Chapter 6: Leaving a Legacy

6.1 Personal Letters and Messages to Loved Ones

Letters addressed to those you leave behind can provide comfort, closure, and a lasting connection. You may write a conventional letter, detailing things you want to say to that person. You might share memories, lessons learned, and expressions of love and gratitude.

They can also be written to be opened at specific dates or events, such as a milestone birthday, the day of a wedding, or the birth of a child. Receiving such a letter can be of emotional significance for family and friends.

Should you need tips on what to write, the following prompts will get you started. You don't have to confine yourself to those if there is anything else you would like to say.

- Important life lessons and values you want to pass on.

- Regrets and apologies.

- Favorite memories shared with the recipient.

- Words of encouragement and support for future challenges.

- Hopes and dreams you have for them.

The letters need to be stored in a safe place, with loved ones knowing how to access them. They could be left with a trusted friend or family member to be delivered at an appropriate time. Another option is to leave them with the executor of your will.

6.2 Digital Legacies: Social Media, Passwords, and Online Memorials

While on the subject of leaving a legacy, you should consider also your digital legacy. This is all the information that you have posted online, and some perhaps that you haven't posted but has found its way there anyway.

This can be in the form of online accounts, social media profiles and digital content (blogs, publications, photos, videos, etc.) You must decide how these assets will be managed after your death. Will they be maintained or deleted, and if so, how and by whom?

Many of your social media and allied online accounts will be password protected, and possibly with two-factor verification. In order to either shut down or manage these accounts, someone will need access to your passwords, and the verification process. A password manager will help in managing your digital legacy. You will need to give access in advance to a trusted person, or leave written instructions with your executor, to be implemented on your passing.

6.3 Creating a Lasting Impact

Other ways of creating a lasting legacy are through supporting charitable causes or organisations that reflect your personal values. You could establish scholarships, foundations, or community initiatives in your name (or you could support existing scholarships, etc.)

Conclusion

You have the ability to shape how you are remembered, both through personal messages and the impact of your actions. Leaving a legacy is a reflection of your life, your values, and your relationships.

Chapter 7: When the Time Comes

Handling the Practical Stuff (For Your Loved Ones)

Provide a checklist of immediate actions for loved ones to take when you away, including:

- Notifying the appropriate authorities (e.g., medical personnel, hospice care).
- Contacting a funeral home or service provider to discuss arrangements.
- Locating important documents (will, advance directives, insurance policies).
- Informing banks, creditors, and other institutions about the passing.
- Reviewing and executing any pre-planned funeral arrangements.
- Leave a list of people you specifically want to be notified. Likewise, you can leave a list of those you would prefer where not invited to participate in any of your funeral or post-death proceedings.

This is not an exclusive list, but it is indicative or those people or organisations that must be notified in the event of a death.

-
- The deceased person's doctor.
- Family members, relatives and friends
- Police in the absence of a doctor who could issue a certificate.
- Funeral Director
- Employer
- Executor of the Will (where applicable)
- Bank or Financial Institutions

It's Your Funeral

- Solicitor
- Union
- Professional Associations and Institutes
- Clubs (e.g. RSL, Masonic, Rotary, Lions, Sporting, Social, Specific Interest, etc.)
- Taxation Department
- Department of Social Security
- Department of Veterans Affairs
- Insurance Company (Life, House, Car, Health, etc.)
- Superannuation Company.
- Health Fund
- Electoral Office
- Library - return any outstanding books
- State Electricity Commission
- Gas and Fuel Company
- Internet Provider
- Telecom
- Cancel newspaper, milk and other deliveries (if appropriate)
- Re-direct mail (if appropriate)
- Cancel regular debits against the credit card or bank account.

Continuing the Legacy:
Discuss how loved ones can continue your legacy, whether through charitable contributions, supporting causes you cared about, or simply sharing stories and memories. Donations can be made to your favourite causes instead of giving floral tributes.

Epilogue – perhaps for you the epitaph

This book provides a guide for you in planning for final curtain, but as you can see, there are many possibilities in making arrangements for your funeral. The concept is up to you, and you can prepare as much or as little as you like.

It discusses some of the issues you need to consider besides the actual ceremony, such as the legalities, a legacy, and tying up any loose ends.

Best of all, it helps you to retain a measure of control over your exit from this life, and to do so with a desire to tell your own story, with care and concern for others, and knowing that you have done the best you can.

It's your funeral.

About the Author

Dorothy Shorne has been a Civil Celebrant since 1994, and has assisted many people to plan funerals for their loved ones. With having been charged with the task of conducting the funeral for her own mother, she understands how important it is that the ceremony acknowledges and celebrates the life of the departed person, whilst meeting the needs of those who are bereaved.

Each ceremony is planned with care after detailed discussion with the bereaved and with regard to the deceased's known wishes.

❊

Under the name of Emily Hussey, she is a published romance writer, and loves the short story format in a range of genres. Dorothy now resides on the coast in the city of Adelaide, and is exploring the writing options in every café in walking distance.

❊

Contact Details: dorothy@shorne.com.au.
Any comments are welcome, and if you leave a review at the place where you purchased this book, I would be delighted.

Also By Dorothy Shorne

Rites of Passage Series

From This Day Forward
It's Your Funeral
Naming Ceremonies
The Last Farewell

❀

Fiction

Skywalkers

❀

Writing as Emily Hussey

Red Centre Series
Tales from Harrow Series
Sandy Bay Series
Maison Angelique
Ambition and Passion
Seasons of the Heart

www.ingramcontent.com/pod-product-compliance
Lightning Source LLC
Chambersburg PA
CBHW071717020426
42333CB00017B/2300